WeightWatchers®

Seasonally Sensational

Utterly delicious recipes using fresh ingredients for every month of the year

SIMON &
SCHUSTER

LONDON · NEW YORK · SYDNEY · TORONTO

First published in Great Britain by Simon & Schuster UK Ltd, 2010
A CBS Company

Weight Watchers Publications Team: Jane Griffiths and Fiona Smith.

A selection of recipes appear courtesy of weightwatchers.co.uk. For more information about Weight Watchers Online visit www.weightwatchers.co.uk

Recipes written by: Sue Ashworth, Sue Beveridge, Tamsin Burnett-Hall, Roz Denny, Nicola Graimes, Becky Johnson, Kim Morphew, Joy Skipper, Penny Stephens and Wendy Veale.

Photography by Iain Bagwell, Steve Baxter, Steve Lee and Juliet Piddington
Design and typesetting by Tiger Media Ltd
Printed and bound in Singapore

A CIP catalogue for this book is available from the British Library

ISBN 978-1-84737-789-0

1 3 5 7 9 10 8 6 4 2

Pictured on the front cover: Spring chicken bake p85.
Pictured on the back cover: Asparagus and leek tart p78, Creamy summery pasta p96, Rich beef and prune casserole p170,
Christmas cranberry muffins p18
Pictured on the introduction: Minty lamb burgers p113, Thai style mussels p56, Asparagus and leek tart p78, Rich beef and prune casserole p170.

 POINTS ® value logo: You'll find this easy to read *POINTS* value logo on every recipe throughout this book. The logo represents the number of *POINTS* values per serving each recipe contains. Weight Watchers offers you a healthy and sustainable way to lose weight. For more information about Weight Watchers call 08457 123 000.

NEW RECIPE This symbol denotes a brand new recipe that has not previously been published.

 This symbol denotes a vegetarian recipe and assumes that, where relevant, free range eggs, vegetarian cheese, vegetarian virtually fat free fromage frais, vegetarian low fat crème fraîche and vegetarian low fat yogurt are used. Virtually fat free fromage frais, low fat crème fraîche and low fat yogurt may contain traces of gelatine so they are not always vegetarian. Please check the labels.

 This symbol denotes a dish that can be frozen.

Recipe notes
Egg size: Medium, unless otherwise stated.
All fruits and vegetables: Medium sized, unless otherwise stated.
Raw eggs: Only the freshest eggs should be used. Pregnant women, the elderly and children should avoid recipes with eggs that are not fully cooked or raw.
Stock: Stock cubes used in recipes, unless otherwise stated. These should be prepared according to packet instructions.
Recipe timings: These are approximate and meant to be guidelines. Please note that the preparation time includes all the steps up to and following the main cooking time(s).
Low fat spread: Where a recipe states to use a low fat spread, a light spread with a fat content of no less than 38%, such as Bertolli Light, Flora Light and Sainsbury's Sunflower Light, should be used.

Contents

Introduction   5

WINTER
December   6
January   20
February   34

SPRING
March   48
April   62
May   76

SUMMER
June   90
July   104
August   118

AUTUMN
September   132
October   146
November   160

Index   174

Introduction

This collection of delicious recipes from Weight Watchers explores the joys of eating seasonally – whether it is fruit, vegetables, meat or fish. Starting in winter, each chapter contains recipes using fresh ingredients that are likely to be in season that month. From wintery cabbage to spring greens, summer fruits to autumnal root vegetables, there are over 100 recipes to try throughout the year, including 20 brand **new** recipes.

Seasonal eating is exciting. Instead of the same old supper month after month, try these recipes through the year and explore new ideas and new ingredients. You may even find a new favourite vegetable or a new way of using a glut of seasonal fruit.

Seasonal eating is not only trendy but also more interesting, good for the environment and good for our farmers. Although some fruits and vegetables are available all year round, by eating seasonally you will generally be eating a wide variety of fresh and tasty foods as they go in and out of season.

So, turn the pages, find the right month and get going. There are so many seasonally sensational recipes here to try.

Winter

December

January
February

Chestnut Soup with Sage and Caraway Croûtons

A rich and warming soup to serve as a seasonal supper party starter or as a warming lunch.

Serves 6 | Takes 10 minutes to prepare, 20 minutes to cook | 18½ *POINTS* values per recipe | 148 calories per serving
Ⓥ if using vegetable stock

1 litre (35 fl oz) hot chicken or vegetable stock
1 leek, sliced
2 carrots, peeled and sliced
1 celery stick, sliced
435 g (15½ oz) unsweetened chestnut purée

For the croûtons
2 medium slices brown bread, crusts removed
low fat cooking spray
16 fresh sage leaves or 2 teaspoons dried sage
½ tablespoon caraway seeds
4 fresh chestnuts, peeled and roughly chopped

1   Add the stock to a large, lidded saucepan and bring to the boil. Add the leek, carrots and celery, cover and simmer for 20 minutes until all the vegetables are tender.

2   Add the chestnut purée then, using a hand held blender or liquidiser, blend until smooth. Return the soup to the pan, bring back to the boil and keep simmering over a low heat until ready to serve.

3   To make the croûtons, cut each slice of bread into 16 squares. Spray a small, non stick frying pan with the cooking spray and heat until sizzling. Add the bread cubes and cook over a medium heat for 2 minutes. Turn the squares over and cook for another minute until golden. Add the sage, caraway seeds and chopped chestnuts and cook, stirring for 1–2 minutes or until the sage leaves begin to toast and the nuts turn golden.

4   Serve the soup in warm bowls topped with the croûtons, sage, seeds and nuts.

Smoked Salmon Pâté

Perfect for parties or as a starter during the holiday season, this pâté is also ideal for taking in a lunch box – simply pack the salad and crispbreads separately. Any leftover pâté will keep in the fridge for several days.

Serves 6 | Takes 10 minutes + chilling | 14½ **POINTS** values per recipe | 110 calories per serving

150 g (5½ oz) smoked salmon pieces
finely grated zest of 1 lemon
1½ tablespoons fresh lemon juice
1 tablespoon horseradish sauce
200 g (7 oz) low fat soft cheese
15 g (½ oz) fresh dill, plus a few sprigs to garnish
freshly ground black pepper

To serve
a selection of zero **POINTS** value salad vegetables
12 rye crispbreads
slices of lemon, to garnish (optional)

1 Place the smoked salmon in a food processor with the lemon zest and juice, horseradish sauce, soft cheese and dill. Whizz until everything is well combined but not completely smooth.

2 Season to taste with black pepper, then spoon into a tub, smooth the top and cover with clingfilm. Transfer to the fridge and chill until you're ready to use. (If you want to be able to slice the pâté, line the tub with clingfilm first so that you can remove the contents easily. Chill for at least 12 hours.)

3 To serve, share out the zero **POINTS** value salad vegetables between six plates and spoon the pâté alongside. If you're slicing it, gently lift the pâté from its container using the clingfilm lining and slice on a plate before transferring to the individual plates. Serve with 2 crispbreads each and garnish with the remaining dill and some lemon slices, if using.

Braised Chicken with Red Cabbage

Serve this delicious winter dish with a 225 g (8 oz) baked potato per person, for an additional 2½ **POINTS** values per serving.

Serves 4 | Takes 20 minutes to prepare, 45 minutes to cook | 16 **POINTS** values per recipe | 224 calories per serving

low fat cooking spray
500 g (1 lb 2 oz) red cabbage, shredded
1 apple, peeled and grated
2 tablespoons wine vinegar
1 tablespoon soy sauce

4 x 150 g (5½ oz) skinless boneless chicken breasts
2 rashers lean back bacon, halved lengthways
300 ml (10 fl oz) chicken stock
2 tablespoons half fat crème fraîche
salt and freshly ground black pepper

1   Preheat the oven to Gas Mark 4/180°C/fan oven 160°C.

2   Heat a large, lidded, non stick frying pan and spray with the cooking spray. Add the cabbage and apple and stir fry for a few seconds, then add the wine vinegar, soy sauce and 3 tablespoons of water. Cover and simmer over a very low heat for 15 minutes or until softened.

3   Meanwhile, wrap each chicken piece with half a rasher of bacon.

4   Transfer the cabbage and apple to an ovenproof dish, arrange the chicken pieces on top, cover with foil and bake for 30 minutes. Remove the foil for the last 10 minutes, to allow the bacon to crisp and brown.

5   Meanwhile, make a sauce by boiling the stock in a small pan until it is reduced by half. Leave to cool until it is warm, add the crème fraîche and whisk in. Season to taste.

6   Serve the chicken on a bed of the cabbage with some of the sauce poured over.

Oriental Style Turkey Leftovers

This is a tasty and unusual way to use up some of the leftover Christmas turkey and vegetables.

Serves 2 | Takes 20 minutes | 4½ *POINTS* values per recipe | 220 calories per serving

200 g (7 oz) cooked turkey meat

low fat cooking spray

2.5 cm (1 inch) piece of fresh root ginger, peeled and
sliced into matchsticks

2 garlic cloves, sliced finely

400 g (14 oz) leftover cooked zero *POINTS* value vegetables,
e.g. Brussels sprouts, shredded; carrots,
sliced finely; cabbage, shredded

1–2 tablespoons soy sauce

1 tablespoon runny honey

2 tablespoons rice vinegar or white wine vinegar

salt and freshly ground black pepper

a small bunch of fresh coriander, parsley or mint,
chopped, to garnish

1 Shred the cooked turkey meat as finely as possible. Heat
a large, non stick frying pan and spray with the cooking
spray. Add the ginger and garlic and stir fry for
2 minutes or until golden.

2 Add the vegetables, turkey, soy sauce, honey, vinegar
and seasoning and stir fry together until thoroughly
heated through. Scatter with the herbs and serve at
once.

Honey and Mustard Pork

These pork steaks, in a delicious sweet-sharp sauce, need nothing more than some green cabbage to go with them for no additional *POINTS* values.

Serves 4 | Takes 25 minutes | 14½ *POINTS* values per recipe | 275 calories per serving

450 g (1 lb) swede, peeled and diced
450 g (1 lb) carrots, peeled and diced
low fat cooking spray
4 x 150 g (5½ oz) lean pork steaks

2 tablespoons honey
2 tablespoons grain mustard
juice of ½ a lemon
salt and freshly ground black pepper

1   Bring a pan of water to the boil and add the diced swede and carrots. Cover and simmer for 15–20 minutes until tender. Drain well, mash roughly and season to taste.

2   When the vegetables have been cooking for about 10 minutes, heat a large, non stick frying pan and spray with the cooking spray. Season the pork steaks and brown for 3–4 minutes on each side, depending on their thickness, or until cooked through.

3   Mix the honey, mustard and lemon juice together and pour over the pork steaks. Cook for 1 minute more or until cooked through, turning the pork steaks to glaze them in the sauce. Serve with the mashed carrot and swede.

Winter Vegetable Casserole with Spicy Dumplings

This recipe is great for warming you up on those cold winter days. Try exchanging some of the zero **POINTS** value vegetables for your own favourites to give it that personal touch.

Serves 4 | Takes 30 minutes to prepare, 40 minutes to cook | 16 **POINTS** values per recipe
306 calories per serving | ⓥ

For the dumplings
90 g (3¼ oz) self raising flour
a pinch of salt
1 teaspoon ground coriander
1 teaspoon cumin seeds
2 tablespoons low fat spread

For the casserole
2 teaspoons vegetable oil
90 g (3¼ oz) shallots or small onions, halved

1 leek, sliced
1 large carrot, peeled and sliced
225 g (8 oz) parsnips, chopped
2 celery sticks, chopped
1.2 litres (2 pints) vegetable stock
25 g (1 oz) pearl barley or bulghar wheat
400 g (14 oz) canned chick peas, rinsed and drained
175 g (6 oz) cauliflower, broken into florets
salt and freshly ground black pepper
a handful of parsley or coriander, to garnish (optional)

1 For the dumplings, sift the flour and salt into a large bowl then mix in the ground coriander and cumin seeds. Rub in the low fat spread until the mixture resembles fine breadcrumbs. Add enough cold water to make a soft, but not sticky, dough. Form into eight dumplings, cover then set aside.

2 Heat the oil in a large, lidded saucepan then sauté the shallots or onions, leek, carrot, parsnips and celery for 5 minutes, without browning them.

3 Add the stock, pearl barley or bulghar wheat and chick peas to the saucepan. Bring to the boil then reduce the heat, cover and simmer for 20 minutes.

4 Add the cauliflower and dumplings to the saucepan. Cover and simmer for 20 minutes or until the dumplings are cooked – they should be light and fluffy.

5 Season the casserole to taste. Serve, garnished with parsley or coriander, if using, allowing two dumplings per person.

Braised Pork Casserole

An ideal recipe for the winter months. This is delicious and indulgent enough to serve on special occasions but still low in *POINTS* values.

Serves 4 | Takes 10 minutes to prepare, 50 minutes to cook | 18½ *POINTS* values per recipe
275 calories per serving (with crème fraîche) | ❋

1 tablespoon vegetable oil
1 large onion, chopped
500 g (1 lb 2 oz) lean pork, cut into 2.5 cm (1 inch) cubes
4 celery sticks, cut into 2 cm (¾ inch) slices
1 large sprig of fresh sage or rosemary
1 medium Bramley apple, peeled, cored and sliced thickly

1 eating apple (e.g. Cox's), cored, peeled and sliced thickly
300 ml (10 fl oz) dry cider or unsweetened apple juice
2 teaspoons cornflour
2 tablespoons half fat crème fraîche (optional)
salt and freshly ground black pepper
1 tablespoon chopped fresh sage or rosemary, to garnish

1 Preheat the oven to Gas Mark 5/190°C/fan oven 170°C. Heat the oil in a lidded, flameproof casserole dish. Add the onion and pork and stir fry until the meat has coloured and the onion softened.

2 Add the celery and fresh herb sprig and toss over the heat for 2–3 minutes. Stir in the apples and cider or apple juice. Season.

3 Cover tightly, transfer to the oven and cook for 50 minutes or until the meat is tender and the apples are beginning to break up.

4 Remove the herb sprig. Blend the cornflour with a drop of water and stir this into the casserole. Transfer the casserole to a moderate heat on the hob and heat until the sauce thickens slightly. Adjust the seasoning to taste.

5 Just before serving, swirl in the crème fraîche, if using, and garnish with the chopped fresh herbs.

Tip

Bramley apples cook down to a pulp very quickly so add an eating apple, which holds its shape well, to get a chunkier texture. This works as well for apple sauce and pie fillings.

Variations

For those of you who like celeriac, replace the celery with 225 g (8 oz) of this delicious vegetable, peeled and cut into 2 cm (¾-inch) chunks.

By omitting the crème fraîche you will reduce your *POINTS* values per serving to 4.

Beef Hotpot

A comforting casserole full of flavoursome root vegetables with a warming hint of wine.

Serves 4 | Takes 30 minutes to prepare, 1 hour to cook | 15 *POINTS* values per recipe
325 calories per serving | ☀

low fat cooking spray
400 g (14 oz) lean stewing steak, cubed
4 onions, chopped
4 garlic cloves, chopped
4 carrots, peeled and chopped into semi-circles
4 parsnips, chopped into semi-circles
4 small swedes or turnips, chopped

a bunch of fresh thyme or 4 sprigs of fresh rosemary,
  leaves only, chopped
400 g can chopped tomatoes
2 tablespoons tomato purée
100 ml (3½ fl oz) red wine (optional)
salt and freshly ground black pepper

1   Spray a large casserole dish with the cooking spray and
    heat until hot. Add the beef, season and brown all over.
    You may need to do this in batches. Remove and set aside.

2   Add the onions and garlic to the dish and cook for
    4 minutes until softened.

3   Return the beef to the casserole with the carrots,
    parsnips, swedes or turnips, herbs, tomatoes, tomato
    purée and red wine, if using. Season and add enough
    water to cover.

4   Bring to the boil, cover and simmer for 1 hour or until
    thick and rich. Serve in warmed bowls.

Baileys Mousse

Light, fluffy and utterly delectable.

Serves 6 | Takes 10 minutes + chilling | 17 **POINTS** values per recipe | 143 calories per serving | Ⓥ

60 g (2 oz) caster sugar
3 eggs, separated
4 tablespoons Baileys Irish Cream

3 tablespoons whipping cream
½ heaped teaspoon cocoa powder (optional)

1 Reserve 1 tablespoon of caster sugar. Place the remaining sugar in a small, heavy based saucepan with 1 tablespoon of water. Heat gently until the sugar dissolves, then boil rapidly for about 1 minute until the mixture is syrupy, but not caramelised.

2 In a clean, grease free bowl, whisk the egg whites until stiff. Slowly add the sugar syrup, beating well to thoroughly combine.

3 Put the egg yolks, reserved sugar and Baileys liqueur in a large heatproof bowl. Position the bowl over a saucepan of gently simmering water and whisk until thick and frothy. This will take at least 5 minutes. Whisk in the egg white mixture.

4 Share the mousse between 6 glasses and chill in the fridge until ready to serve.

5 Whisk the whipping cream until it holds its shape. Use to top the desserts, then serve at once, sprinkled with the cocoa powder (if using).

Variation

Try making this using Tia Maria instead of Baileys, for 2½ **POINTS** values per serving.

Christmas Cranberry Muffins

Great for the party season, these delicious muffins taste wonderful and are low in **POINTS** values.

Makes 12 muffins | Takes 10 minutes to prepare, 20 minutes to cook | 31½ **POINTS** values per recipe
135 calories per serving | ♥

1 egg
75 g (2¾ oz) low fat spread, melted
100 g (3½ oz) low fat natural yogurt
100 ml (3½ fl oz) cranberry and apple juice from a carton
75 g (2¾ oz) dried cranberries
100 g (3½ oz) fresh or frozen cranberries, defrosted

50 g (1¾ oz) soft brown sugar
200 g (7 oz) self raising flour
½ teaspoon bicarbonate of soda
1 teaspoon ground cinnamon
2 teaspoons demerara sugar

1 Preheat the oven to Gas Mark 4/180°C/fan oven 160°C and put 12 muffin cases into a 12 cup muffin tin (or use 2 x 6 cup muffin tins).

2 In a large bowl or measuring jug, whisk together the egg, low fat spread, yogurt, juice and dried and fresh (or thawed) cranberries.

3 In another large bowl, stir together the sugar, flour, bicarbonate of soda and cinnamon.

4 Pour the liquid ingredients into the dry ingredients and work quickly to lightly fold them together with a large metal spoon.

5 Immediately and speedily, as speed is essential if the muffins are to rise well, spoon the mixture into the prepared cases and sprinkle each muffin with a pinch of demerara sugar.

6 Bake for 15–20 minutes, or until risen and golden and the tops spring back to the touch.

7 Allow to cool for a few minutes then serve warm or, once cool, keep in an airtight container for up to 2 days.

Winter

December
January
February

Creamy Celeriac Soup

A wonderful, filling soup that makes a really satisfying lunch – perfect for those days when you want to feel full but have very few *POINTS* values to spare.

Serves 4 I Takes 25 minutes I 4½ *POINTS* values per recipe I 90 calories per serving I 🅥 I ❄

600 ml (1 pint) boiling water
600 g (1 lb 5 oz) celeriac, peeled and cut into small chunks
200 g (7 oz) potatoes, peeled and cut into small chunks
1 vegetable stock cube
¼ teaspoon garlic granules

1 tablespoon lemon juice
300 ml (10 fl oz) semi skimmed milk
½ teaspoon celery salt
salt and freshly ground black pepper
1 tablespoon chopped parsley, to garnish

1   In a large, lidded pan, pour the boiling water over the chopped vegetables. Add the stock cube, garlic granules and lemon juice, stir and bring to the boil. Don't worry if the water doesn't completely cover the vegetables, but make sure you stir them regularly so that they cook evenly. Cover the pan and simmer gently for 15–20 minutes or until the vegetables are tender.

2   Using a food processor or hand held blender, whizz the soup to a thick purée. Add the milk and celery salt and return to the heat. Gently warm through and season to taste. Serve in warmed soup bowls sprinkled with the parsley.

Tips

Be extra careful when reheating thick soups like this one. They tend to splutter suddenly from the pan when they start to boil and can scald you.

Garlic granules are readily available from supermarkets, in the same section as all the other dried herbs and spices.

Variation

For an even creamier version, use the same quantity of whole milk instead of semi skimmed milk, for 1½ *POINTS* values per serving.

Peppered Steak with Balsamic Onions

Try this mouth-watering recipe for a special occasion.

Serves 2 I Takes 30 minutes I 12½ **POINTS** values per recipe I 421 calories per serving

500 g (1 lb 2 oz) potatoes, peeled and diced
½ beef stock cube
low fat cooking spray
1 large onion, sliced thinly

2 tablespoons balsamic vinegar
1 tablespoon redcurrant jelly
2 x 110 g (4 oz) fillet or medallion steaks
salt and freshly ground black pepper

1   Preheat the oven to Gas Mark 7/220°C/fan oven 200°C.
    Bring a pan of water to the boil and add the potatoes and
    beef stock cube. Cook for 4 minutes then drain
    (reserving the stock) and tip on to a non stick baking tray.

2   Spread the potatoes out, lightly spray with the cooking
    spray and cook in the oven for 20–25 minutes until
    crisp and golden.

3   Meanwhile, heat a non stick, lidded pan, spray with the
    cooking spray and fry the onion for 5 minutes over a
    high heat, until browned. Add the balsamic vinegar and
    6 tablespoons of the reserved stock. Cover the pan and
    cook for 20 minutes until tender. Stir in the redcurrant
    jelly until melted.

4   Season the steaks generously. Heat a non stick frying
    pan and cook for 3–4 minutes on each side, or until
    done to your liking. Serve with the roasted potatoes
    and sticky onions.

Spiced Cauliflower Pasta

This is a very unusual way to cook cauliflower, but once you've tried it you'll try it again and again.

Serves 4 | Takes 25 minutes | 20 *POINTS* values per recipe | 395 calories per serving | Ⓥ

1 large cauliflower, cut into florets
2 tablespoons ground cumin
1 tablespoon ground cinnamon
350 g (12 oz) dried pasta

300 g (10½ oz) low fat natural yogurt
1 packet fresh coriander or mint, chopped finely
salt and freshly ground black pepper

1 Preheat the oven to Gas Mark 8/230°C/fan oven 210°C. On a non stick baking tray, toss the cauliflower florets in the cumin and cinnamon. Roast in the oven for 20 minutes or until softened and slightly charred.

2 Meanwhile, bring a pan of water to the boil and cook the pasta according to the packet instructions. Drain.

3 Toss the pasta with the cooked cauliflower and stir in the yogurt, coriander or mint and seasoning. Serve immediately.

Fish Pie

This fish pie has a rosti-style grated potato topping instead of the usual mash.

Serves 4 | Takes 30 minutes to prepare, 25 minutes to cook | 26 *POINTS* values per recipe
423 calories per serving | ❄ (before cooking)

500 g (1 lb 2 oz) smoked haddock
600 ml (20 fl oz) skimmed milk
2 bay leaves
750 g (1 lb 10 oz) potatoes, roughly the same size
300 g (10½ oz) cooked, peeled prawns

40 g (1½ oz) low fat spread
50 g (1¾ oz) plain flour
1 tablespoon lemon juice
1 tablespoon chopped fresh parsley
salt and freshly ground black pepper

1   Preheat the oven to Gas Mark 4/180°C/fan oven 160°C.

2   Place the smoked haddock in a roasting tin, pour in the milk, add the bay leaves and bake in the oven for 15 minutes or until the fish flakes easily.

3   Meanwhile, bring a pan of water to the boil and cook the unpeeled potatoes for 8 minutes. Drain and leave to cool slightly.

4   Reserving the milk, lift the fish on to a plate then break into flakes using a fork, discarding any skin and bones. Transfer to a baking dish and mix with the prawns.

5   Place the low fat spread and flour in a non stick saucepan and gradually blend in the fishy milk. Bring to a simmer, stirring until smooth, then simmer for 3 minutes. Add the lemon juice, parsley and seasoning to taste. Remove the bay leaves and pour the milk into the baking dish.

6   Scrape the skins from the potatoes then coarsely grate the potatoes straight over the baking dish to form an even topping.

7   Bake for 25 minutes until crisp and golden.

Chicken, Leek and Sweetcorn Cobbler

NEW RECIPE

A savoury cobbler makes a delicious change from the traditional pastry topped pie. The cobbler topping is essentially a savoury scone mixture. Serve with carrots and green cabbage, for no additional *POINTS* values.

Serves 4 | Takes 20 minutes to prepare. 20 minutes to cook | 22½ *POINTS* values per recipe | 378 calories per serving

low fat cooking spray
400 g (14 oz) skinless boneless chicken breast, diced
2 leeks, sliced
25 g (1 oz) plain flour
300 ml (10 fl oz) hot chicken stock
150 ml (5 fl oz) skimmed milk, plus 1 teaspoon to glaze
150 g (5½ oz) frozen sweetcorn

For the cobbler
150 g (5½ oz) self raising flour
a pinch of salt
60 g (2 oz) low fat spread
1 tablespoon snipped fresh chives
4 tablespoons low fat natural yogurt
freshly ground black pepper

1 Preheat the oven to Gas Mark 4/180°C/fan oven 160°C. Heat a non stick frying pan until hot and spray with the cooking spray. Cook the chicken for 3 minutes until starting to brown, add the leeks and cook for another 2 minutes.

2 Stir in the flour to coat the chicken and leeks, then gradually blend in the stock and milk. Bring to the boil and simmer for 5 minutes. Stir the sweetcorn into the sauce then pour the filling into an ovenproof dish.

3 To make the cobbler, reserve 1 tablespoon of the flour for rolling out then sift the rest into a mixing bowl with a pinch of salt. Season with black pepper and, using your fingertips, rub in the low fat spread until the mixture resembles breadcrumbs. Stir in the chives then add the yogurt to bind to a soft but not sticky dough, adding a little water if needed.

4 Dust the work surface with the reserved flour and pat the dough out to 1 cm (½ inch) thick. Using a cutter, stamp out twelve 5 cm (2 inch) rounds, re-rolling as needed, and place on top of the chicken filling. Brush the rounds with 1 teaspoon of milk to glaze then bake in the oven for 20 minutes until the cobbler topping is risen and golden brown.

🅥 Variation

For a vegetarian alternative, replace the diced chicken with 500 g (1 lb 2 oz) button mushrooms. Use vegetable stock instead of the chicken stock when making the sauce, for 4 *POINTS* values per serving.

Gammon in Raisin Sauce

Although raisin sauce sounds a bit unusual, rest assured – it is absolutely delicious.

Serves 4 I Takes 10 minutes to prepare, 30 minutes to cook I 17 *POINTS* values per recipe I 260 calories per serving

500 g (1 lb 2 oz) smoked gammon steaks, about
  1 cm (½-inch) thick
low fat cooking spray
1 onion, chopped finely
2 tablespoons raisins
8 thin strips of orange peel

300 ml (10 fl oz) dry cider
1 tablespoon cornflour
150 ml (5 fl oz) fresh orange juice
freshly ground black pepper

1   Cut each gammon slice into four equal pieces and remove the rind and the fat.

2   Spray a large, heavy based, non stick frying pan with the cooking spray and heat for a few moments. Add the gammon pieces, searing them on both sides.

3   Add the onion, raisins, orange peel and cider. Heat, then cover and simmer for 25–30 minutes.

4   Blend the cornflour into the orange juice. Lift the gammon from the frying pan and keep warm. Stir the orange juice mixture into the pan and heat until thickened. Bubble for a few moments, then season with pepper and serve with the gammon.

Variation

You could use unsweetened apple juice instead of cider. The *POINTS* values will remain the same.

Winter Pork Ragu

This rich and tasty ragu with coconut, almonds, apricots and spices is perfect for a cold winter's evening.

Serves 4 | Takes 30 minutes to prepare, 40 minutes to cook | 22½ *POINTS* values per recipe

305 calories per serving | ❋

low fat cooking spray

500 g (1 lb 2 oz) lean pork tenderloin, cut into
   2 cm (¾ inch) cubes

1 onion, chopped finely

1 teaspoon ground cinnamon

¼ teaspoon grated nutmeg

1 star anise

1 tablespoon plain flour

1 red chilli, de-seeded and chopped finely

2 cm (¾ inch) piece of fresh root ginger, peeled and grated

25 g (1 oz) whole blanched almonds

600 ml (20 fl oz) vegetable stock

1 tablespoon tomato purée

100 ml (3½ fl oz) reduced fat coconut milk

50 g (1¾ oz) ready to eat dried apricots, halved

25 g packet of fresh coriander, chopped roughly

salt and freshly ground black pepper

1   Heat a large, lidded, heavy based saucepan and spray with the cooking spray. Add the pork in batches and cook for 1 minute on each side until brown. Transfer to a plate and set aside.

2   Spray the pan again with the cooking spray and gently cook the onion for 3–4 minutes until softened. Add the cinnamon, nutmeg, star anise, flour, chilli, ginger and almonds. Return the pork to the saucepan and cook for 2 minutes, stirring constantly.

3   Pour in the vegetable stock, tomato purée and coconut milk. Bring to the boil, cover and simmer for 35 minutes, stirring from time to time. Stir in the apricots and cook gently for 5 minutes. Check the seasoning, stir in the coriander and serve.

Jewelled Clementine Pavlova

This pavlova makes a fabulous finale to any special meal. Make the meringue base the day before if you like, then store in an airtight tin or wrap in clingfilm.

Serves 12 | Takes 25 minutes to prepare, 3 hours to cook + cooling | 32½ *POINTS* values per recipe
136 calories per serving | ◉

4 egg whites
225 g (8 oz) caster sugar
150 ml (5 fl oz) whipping cream

5 clementines or tangerines, peeled and segmented
1 pomegranate

1   Preheat the oven to Gas Mark 1/140°C/fan oven 120°C. Line a baking tray with non stick baking parchment and draw a 30 cm (12 inch) circle on it.

2   In a large grease free bowl, and using a hand held electric whisk, whisk the egg whites until they hold their shape. Gradually add the sugar, whisking well until the egg whites are stiff and glossy.

3   Spread the meringue mixture in an even layer over the marked out circle. Bake in the oven for 2–3 hours. The meringue will be dried out rather than cooked at this low temperature. Leave to cool completely.

4   Whip the cream until it holds its shape. Spread on top of the meringue. Cut the pomegranate in half and remove the seeds. Arrange the clementine or tangerine segments on top of the cream and scatter with the pomegranate seeds.

Tip

Remember that egg whites will not whip if there is any trace of grease in the bowl or on the beaters (including egg yolk).

Rum Caramelised Oranges

NEW RECIPE

A taste of the Caribbean in a bowl.

Serves 4 | Takes 10 minutes | 10½ *POINTS* values per recipe | 212 calories per serving | Ⓥ

4 large oranges
3 tablespoons dark rum
40 g (1½ oz) Demerara sugar

½ teaspoon ground cinnamon
freshly grated nutmeg
4 x 60 g (2 oz) scoops low fat vanilla ice cream

1   Preheat the grill to high and line the grill pan with a large sheet of foil, folding the edges up so that they will hold in the aromatic juices.

2   Use a serrated knife to slice the peel away from the oranges and then cut each one into six slices. Arrange the orange slices on the grill pan in a single, close packed layer and drizzle with the rum. Mix the sugar, cinnamon and several gratings of nutmeg together, then sprinkle over the oranges.

3   Grill for 5 minutes or until slightly caramelised. Divide between four bowls, spooning in the juices from the tray. Serve immediately, topped with the ice cream.

Winter

December
January
February

Curried Parsnip Soup

A warming soup for cold days. Serve for lunch or as a starter or freeze portions to have on standby.

Serves 6 | Takes 25 minutes to prepare, 30 minutes to cook | 8 *POINTS* values per recipe
115 calories per serving | Ⓥ | ❋

low fat cooking spray
1 onion, chopped roughly
2 garlic cloves, chopped
1 tablespoon coriander seeds, crushed
1 teaspoon mild curry powder
1 carrot, peeled and chopped

750 g (1 lb 10 oz) parsnips, peeled and cut into chunks
1 litre (35 fl oz) vegetable stock
175 ml (6 fl oz) low alcohol white wine
salt and freshly ground black pepper
chopped fresh coriander, to garnish

1 Heat a large saucepan and spray with the cooking spray. Cook the onion and garlic for 3–4 minutes until softened. Add the coriander seeds and curry powder and cook for 1 minute.

2 Add the carrot, parsnips, vegetable stock and white wine. Bring to the boil. Reduce the heat and simmer for 30 minutes or until the vegetables are tender. Leave to cool slightly.

3 Carefully whizz the soup in a blender, or use a hand held blender, until smooth. Return to the pan, season and gently warm through. Serve in warmed bowls with the coriander to garnish.

Cauliflower Cheese

A time honoured vegetable dish.

Serves 4 | Takes 20 minutes to prepare, 20 minutes to cook **|** 16 *POINTS* values per recipe
245 calories per serving **|** Ⓥ

---

1 large cauliflower, broken into florets
2 bay leaves
50 g (1¾ oz) low fat spread
50 g (1¾ oz) plain flour
300 ml (10 fl oz) skimmed milk
300 ml (10 fl oz) vegetable stock

1 teaspoon Dijon mustard
15 g (½ oz) Parmesan cheese, grated
100 g (3½ oz) mature reduced fat cheese, grated
2 spring onions, sliced
15 g (½ oz) fresh breadcrumbs
salt and freshly ground black pepper

1 Preheat the oven to Gas Mark 6/200°C/fan oven 180°C.

2 Bring a large pan of water to the boil and add the cauliflower florets and bay leaves. Simmer for 5 minutes until tender, then drain well in a colander. Transfer to an ovenproof dish and discard the bay leaves.

3 Place the low fat spread in a non stick saucepan with the flour, milk and vegetable stock. Bring to the boil, whisking until thickened, then simmer for 3 minutes.

4 Remove from the heat and stir in the mustard, Parmesan and 80 g (3 oz) of the reduced fat cheese. Season to taste and pour over the cauliflower.

5 Mix the spring onions with the breadcrumbs and remaining reduced fat cheese and scatter over the cauliflower.

6 Bake in the oven for 15–20 minutes until browned and crisp.

Beef Rogan Josh

Serve this spicy, warming curry with some zero **POINTS** value vegetables, such as in season purple sprouting brocoli, for a feast of colour and taste.

Serves 4 | Takes 25 minutes to prepare, 45 minutes to cook | 17 **POINTS** values per recipe
290 calories per serving | ❋

600 g (1 lb 5 oz) lean beef brisket, cubed
1 teaspoon hot chilli powder
low fat cooking spray
2 onions, sliced thinly
2 garlic cloves, chopped
4 cardamom pods, split

2 bay leaves
2 tablespoons rogan josh curry powder
5 tablespoons canned chopped tomatoes
150 g (5½ oz) low fat natural yogurt
1 medium red chilli, de-seeded and sliced, to garnish

1 Put the beef in a bowl with the chilli powder and turn the meat until coated.

2 Heat a large, lidded, heavy based saucepan, spray with the cooking spray and fry the onions for 7 minutes until softened, adding a little water if they start to stick. Spray again with the cooking spray, then toss in the beef and fry over a medium heat for 2 minutes until the meat is sealed and browned all over.

3 Add the garlic, cardamom, bay leaves and curry powder and cook, stirring, for 30 seconds. Add 1 litre (1¾ pints) water, the tomatoes and yogurt. Stir and bring to the boil. Reduce the heat and simmer, covered, for 45 minutes.

4 Remove the lid and cook, stirring occasionally, until the sauce has reduced and thickened. Serve topped with the sliced red chilli.

Cannelloni

Serve this cannelloni with a large, mixed winter salad with a fat free dressing for no extra *POINTS* values.

Serves 4 | Takes 30 minutes to prepare, 45 minutes to cook | 22 *POINTS* values per recipe
365 calories per serving | ❋

225 g (8 oz) lean pork mince
1 small onion, chopped finely
1 garlic clove, crushed
1 teaspoon mixed dried Italian herbs
1 pork or chicken stock cube, dissolved in 150 ml (5 fl oz) hot water
1 tablespoon cornflour, blended with 2–3 tablespoons cold water

200 g tub low fat soft cheese with garlic and herbs
150 g (5½ oz) low fat natural yogurt
25 g (1 oz) Parmesan cheese, finely grated
low fat cooking spray
320 g jar spicy tomato pasta sauce
16 x 150 g (5½ oz) cannelloni tubes (no pre-cooking required)
salt and freshly ground black pepper

1   Heat a large, non stick frying pan, add the pork mince a handful at a time and cook to seal and brown it.

2   Add the onion and garlic and cook for a minute or two. Add the dried herbs and stock, simmer for 10 minutes, then add the blended cornflour. Cook, stirring until thickened. Season and leave to cool for about 10 minutes.

3   In a mixing bowl, beat the soft cheese with a wooden spoon to soften it. Stir in the yogurt, half the Parmesan cheese and a little seasoning.

4   Preheat the oven to Gas Mark 4/180°C/fan oven 160°C.

5   Spray a shallow, ovenproof dish with the cooking spray. Pour half the tomato pasta sauce into the dish. Spoon the mince mixture into the cannelloni tubes. Arrange the tubes in the baking dish and pour over the remaining pasta sauce. Top with the soft cheese mixture and sprinkle with the remaining Parmesan cheese.

6   Bake for 40–45 minutes, until golden brown and bubbling.

Variation

Try using the same amount of turkey mince instead of pork, for the same *POINTS* values per serving.

Ⓥ **Variation**

For a vegetarian alternative, use 225 g (8 oz) Quorn mince instead of pork, for the same *POINTS* values per serving.

Roast Beef with Yorkshires

A wonderful mixture of caramelised vegetables surround this joint of roast beef, absorbing all the flavours as they cook. Accompanied by crisp Yorkshire puddings and gravy, this is a Sunday roast to remember.

Serves 6 | Takes 20 minutes to prepare, 1½ hours to cook | 44½ **POINTS** values per recipe | 377 calories per serving

1 kg (2 lb 4 oz) joint topside or top rump of beef
350 g (12 oz) baby carrots, scrubbed
250 g (9 oz) parsnips, peeled and cut into chunks
500 g (1 lb 2 oz) potatoes, peeled and cut into chunks
1 red and 1 white onion, each cut into 6 wedges through the root
1 tablespoon clear honey
1 tablespoon wholegrain mustard
salt and freshly ground black pepper

For the Yorkshire puddings
60 g (2 oz) plain flour
1 egg, beaten
150 ml (5 fl oz) skimmed milk
low fat cooking spray

For the gravy
600 ml (20 fl oz) beef stock
1½ tablespoons cornflour, blended with a little cold water

1 Preheat the oven to Gas Mark 5/190°C/fan oven 170°C. Season the beef and place in a large roasting tin. Roast in the oven for 20 minutes initially.

2 Meanwhile, toss the carrots, parsnips, potatoes and onions together with seasoning in a large bowl.

3 Make the Yorkshire pudding batter by sifting the flour into a bowl. Season, then gradually whisk in the egg and milk to form a smooth batter. Transfer to a jug, cover and leave to stand.

4 When the beef has had its initial cooking time, lift it out on to a plate, then tip the vegetables into the tin and stir to coat in the roasting juices. Return the beef to the tin and roast for 30 minutes more, stirring the vegetables around once or twice.

5 Mix the honey and mustard together and brush this over the beef, then cook for a final 10 minutes. When the beef is ready, transfer it to a warmed serving platter, cover with foil and leave to rest.

6 Increase the oven temperature to Gas Mark 7/220°C/fan oven 200°C and return the vegetables to the oven to cook for a further 10 minutes. Pop a 12 hole, non stick bun or Yorkshire pudding tin in the oven to preheat for 5 minutes.

7 When the bun tin is hot, remove from the oven and lightly spray each hollow with the cooking spray. Quickly pour the Yorkshire pudding batter into the hollows, then place on the top shelf of the oven and cook for 12–15 minutes until well risen and crisp.

8 Once the vegetables are tender and caramelised, lift out on to the beef serving platter using a slotted spoon. Spoon any fat out of the roasting tin and pour in the beef stock. Place the roasting tin on the hob, using an oven glove to hold it, and bubble for 5 minutes, scraping up the delicious caramelised bits from the bottom of the tin. Mix in the cornflour paste and stir until the gravy has thickened. Transfer to a warmed jug.

9 Slice the beef thinly, then serve three medium slices of roast beef per person with two Yorkshire puddings, the vegetables and gravy.

Lemongrass and Lime Herby Chicken Kebabs

Create a sensation with these delicious chicken kebabs – though do allow time for the chicken to marinate for the best flavour.

Serves 4 | Takes 10 minutes to prepare + 30 minutes marinating, 10 minutes to cook | 24 *POINTS* values per recipe
393 calories per serving

2 tablespoons soy sauce
1 lemongrass stem, very finely chopped
zest and juice of a lime
1 garlic clove, crushed
2 tablespoons fresh coriander, chopped
4 x 150 g (5½ oz) skinless boneless chicken breasts, cut into chunks

salt and freshly ground black pepper

To serve
250 g (9 oz) easy cook rice
4 lime wedges
coriander sprigs

1   In a bowl, mix together the soy sauce, lemongrass, lime zest and juice, garlic and chopped coriander. Add the chunks of chicken and season. Mix well, then cover and refrigerate for at least 30 minutes to marinate.

2   Meanwhile, soak eight wooden kebab sticks in hot water to prevent them from burning. Bring a pan of water to the boil and cook the rice according to the packet instructions. Preheat the grill to high.

3   Thread the chicken pieces onto the soaked kebab sticks. Grill for 8–10 minutes, turning often. Make sure that the chicken is thoroughly cooked – there should be no trace of pink juices. Cook for a few minutes more, if necessary.

4   Drain the rice and serve with the chicken kebabs, garnished with the lime wedges and coriander sprigs.

Tip

You can buy prepared lemongrass in tubes or small jars, either alongside the fresh herbs or in the spice section at the supermarket. Refrigerate and keep for up to 6 weeks once opened.

Italian Fish Stew

This is a great fish stew, quick to make and full of flavour.

Serves 4 | Takes 15 minutes to prepare plus soaking, 30 minutes to cook | 6½ **POINTS** values per recipe
180 calories per serving

a pinch of saffron strands
low fat cooking spray
1 large onion, chopped finely
2 garlic cloves, crushed
2 red peppers in brine, chopped
2 x 400 g cans chopped tomatoes
300 ml (10 fl oz) vegetable stock
2 bay leaves

a small bunch of basil, chopped
½ teaspoon Tabasco sauce
1 tablespoon tomato purée
450 g (1 lb) cod fillets, skinned and cut into even, bite size chunks
8 large cooked prawns, shelled
salt and freshly ground black pepper

1 Put the saffron strands in a small bowl, add a few tablespoons of boiling water and leave to soak for 30 minutes.

2 Heat a large, lidded, non stick saucepan and spray with the cooking spray. Stir fry the onion and garlic for 5 minutes or until the onion has softened, adding a little water if they start to stick.

3 Stir in the peppers and tomatoes and add the stock, saffron strands with the soaking liquid, bay leaves, half the basil, Tabasco sauce, tomato purée and seasoning. Bring to the boil and simmer for 20 minutes

4 Add the cod and cook, covered, for a further 5 minutes. Then gently fold in the prawns and allow them to heat through. Check the seasoning and scatter with the remaining basil to serve.

St Valentine's Day Seafood and Tomato Pasta

Easy to prepare, using fresh or frozen seafood, this is something special for someone special.

Serves 2 | Takes 35 minutes | 12 **POINTS** values per recipe | 500 calories per serving

200 g (7 oz) dried spaghetti or linguini
low fat cooking spray
1 onion, sliced finely
400 g can chopped tomatoes
2 tablespoons capers, rinsed and drained
200 g (7 oz) seafood selection (prawns, baby squid, scallops, mussels etc.), fresh or frozen and defrosted

1 tablespoon Worcestershire sauce
1–2 drops Tabasco sauce (optional)
salt and freshly ground black pepper
a small bunch of fresh parsley, chopped, to garnish

1   Bring a pan of water to the boil and cook the pasta according to the packet instructions.

2   Meanwhile, heat a large, non stick frying pan until hot, spray with the cooking spray and fry the onion for 5 minutes, until it is softened, adding a few tablespoons of water if it starts to stick.

3   Add the tomatoes, capers and seasoning and stir together. Bring to the boil and simmer for 10 minutes or until the sauce is thickened.

4   Add the seafood, Worcestershire sauce and Tabasco sauce, if using. Stir and cook for a further 3 minutes.

5   Drain the pasta, reserving about 4 tablespoons of the cooking liquid. Toss the pasta with the sauce and the reserved cooking liquid then sprinkle with the fresh parsley and serve.

Orange Sweetheart Cookies

These little cookies can be cut into whatever shape you choose – try hearts for Valentine's Day.

Makes 24 | Takes 20 minutes to prepare + 2 hours chilling, 10 minutes to cook | 31 *POINTS* values per recipe
81 calories per serving | ❤

125 g (4½ oz) low fat spread
125 g (4½ oz) light brown sugar
1 egg
1 teaspoon baking powder
zest of an orange

2 tablespoons orange juice
1 teaspoon vanilla essence
250 g (9 oz) plain flour
icing sugar, to decorate

1 In a large bowl, mix together the low fat spread, sugar, egg, baking powder, orange zest and juice and vanilla essence. Beat with an electric whisk or hand whisk until fluffy.

2 Stir in the flour until well mixed and then chill the mixture for up to 2 hours, until firm. (This may not be necessary – it depends on the temperature of the low fat spread and whether the dough is too soft and sticky to roll out).

3 Preheat the oven to Gas Mark 6/200°C/fan oven 180°C and line two baking trays with non stick baking parchment.

4 Roll or pat out the dough on a floured surface, cut into shapes and transfer to the baking tray with a palette knife.

5 Bake for 6–10 minutes until golden around the edges. Remove from the oven and leave to cool on a wire rack before dusting with icing sugar to decorate.

March

April
May

Pork Tenderloin with Rhubarb Chutney

We teamed up sweet spices like cinnamon, ginger and cloves with naturally tart rhubarb for a unique flavour combination you're sure to love.

Serves 4 | Takes 15 minutes to prepare, 40 minutes to cook | 14 **POINTS** values per recipe | 260 calories per serving

450 g (1 lb) lean pork tenderloin
½ teaspoon ground cinnamon
½ teaspoon ground ginger
¼ teaspoon ground cloves
low fat cooking spray
salt and freshly ground black pepper

For the chutney
2 tablespoons red wine vinegar
35 g (1¼ oz) raisins
85 g (3 oz) strawberry jam
240 g (8¾ oz) rhubarb, chopped

1 Preheat the oven to Gas Mark 4/180°C/fan oven 160°C. Mix together the cinnamon, ginger, cloves and seasoning and rub all over the pork.

2 Place a non stick, ovenproof frying pan over a high heat and spray with the cooking spray. Add the pork and sear on all sides. Transfer the pan to the oven and bake until cooked through, about 25–30 minutes.

3 While the pork is cooking, make the chutney. In a small saucepan, stir together the vinegar, raisins, jam and rhubarb. Bring to a simmer over a medium heat and cook until the rhubarb is very tender, about 10 minutes.

4 To serve, carve the pork into 5 mm (¼ inch) thick slices and top with the rhubarb chutney.

Tip

If you don't have an ovenproof frying pan, use a regular non stick pan and transfer the pork to a non stick baking tray to cook in the oven.

Crisp Coated Fish with Chips

NEW RECIPE

Golden polenta makes a fabulously crunchy coating for white fish fillets.

Serves 4 | Takes 20 minutes to prepare, 30–35 minutes to cook | 24 *POINTS* values per recipe | 455 calories per serving

500 g (1 lb 2 oz) baking potatoes, peeled
500 g (1 lb 2 oz) sweet potatoes, peeled
low fat cooking spray
2 tablespoons plain flour, seasoned
1 egg

2 tablespoons skimmed milk
60 g (2 oz) dried polenta
finely grated zest of ½ a lemon
1 tablespoon finely chopped fresh parsley (optional)
4 x 125 g (4½ oz) skinless pollock fillets

1   Preheat the oven to Gas Mark 6/200°C/fan oven 180°C. Place a large, shallow, non stick roasting tray in the oven to preheat.

2   Cut both types of potato into finger width chips. Bring a lidded pan of water to the boil, add the baking potatoes, cover and cook for 3 minutes. Add the sweet potatoes, cover again and cook for another 3 minutes. Drain well.

3   Remove the hot tray from the oven, spray with the cooking spray and spread the chips out in a single layer. Spray again with the cooking spray and bake in the oven for 20 minutes.

4   Meanwhile, place the seasoned flour on one plate, beat the egg and milk in a shallow dish and mix the polenta with the lemon zest and parsley (if using) on another plate. Dip the fish fillets in the flour, then in the egg and finally in the polenta to coat on all sides.

5   When the 20 minutes is up, add the coated fish to the tray of chips and cook together for 15 minutes until crisp and lightly browned.

Vegetarian Shepherd's Pie

A delicious meatless shepherd's pie for all the family.

Serves 4 | Takes 40 minutes to prepare, 45 minutes to cook | 16½ **POINTS** values per recipe
340 calories per serving | Ⓥ | ❄

500 g (1 lb 2 oz) sweet potato, peeled and cut into
  even chunks
low fat cooking spray
1 onion, chopped finely
2 garlic cloves, crushed
1 celery stick, diced finely
1 carrot, peeled and diced finely
1 tablespoon chopped fresh rosemary leaves

125 ml (4 fl oz) red wine
350 g packet Quorn mince
1 tablespoon plain flour
700 g jar passata
220 g can butter beans, drained and rinsed
25 g (1 oz) reduced fat Cheddar cheese, grated
salt and freshly ground black pepper

1 Put the sweet potato into a lidded pan and cover with cold water. Bring to the boil, cover and simmer for 20 minutes. Drain, mash and season.

2 Meanwhile, preheat the oven to Gas Mark 5/190°C/fan oven 170°C. Heat a non stick saucepan and spray with the cooking spray. Gently fry the onion, garlic, celery, carrot and rosemary for 5–8 minutes until beginning to soften. Add the red wine and bubble for 2 minutes to reduce.

3 Stir in the Quorn mince and flour. Pour in the passata and cook for 5 minutes. Stir through the butter beans, check the seasoning and transfer to a 1 litre (1¾ pint) ovenproof dish.

4 Top the Quorn mince with the mash, spreading evenly with a fork. Sprinkle over the cheese and bake in the oven for 40–45 minutes until golden and bubbling.

Cheat's Chicken Makhani

This cheat's version of chicken makhani (butter chicken) might be low in **POINTS** values, but it's fabulously rich tasting. Accompany with a mini (54 g) naan bread per person, for an extra 3 **POINTS** values, to mop up the flavoursome sauce.

Serves 2 | Takes 20 minutes | 7½ **POINTS** values per recipe | 291 calories per serving

230 g can chopped tomatoes
1 teaspoon tomato purée
1 teaspoon grated fresh root ginger
2 garlic cloves, crushed
¼ teaspoon hot chilli powder
200 ml (7 fl oz) chicken stock

15 g (½ oz) ground almonds
1 teaspoon caster sugar
225 g packet chicken tikka breast pieces
1 tablespoon low fat spread
½ teaspoon garam masala

1 Place the chopped tomatoes, tomato purée, ginger, garlic, chilli powder and chicken stock in a saucepan. Simmer briskly, uncovered, for 10 minutes to reduce.

2 Stir in the ground almonds, sugar and tikka chicken pieces. Gently heat through for 7 minutes, then stir in the low fat spread and garam masala. Serve straightaway.

Thai Style Mussels

Fresh mussels are in season right now, so make the most of them with this zingy dish.

Serves 2 | Takes 20 minutes | 5½ *POINTS* values per recipe | 372 calories per serving

low fat cooking spray
1 onion, chopped
2 garlic cloves, chopped
1 tablespoon Thai red curry paste
175 ml (6 fl oz) hot fish or vegetable stock

75 ml (3 fl oz) dry white wine
juice of a lime
800 g (1 lb 11 oz) cleaned and prepared fresh mussels
2 tablespoons chopped fresh coriander

1 Heat a large, lidded saucepan, spray with the cooking spray and fry the onion for 6 minutes until softened. Add the garlic and cook for another minute.

2 Dissolve the Thai red curry paste in the hot stock and pour it into the pan. Add the wine. Bring to the boil then reduce the heat and simmer, half covered, for 2 minutes.

3 Stir in half of the lime juice then add the mussels, cover and cook over a medium heat for 3 minutes, shaking the pan occasionally.

4 Add the rest of the lime juice and half the coriander, stir well, then cover and cook for a further 1–2 minutes or until the mussels have opened. Discard any mussels that do not open.

5 Serve in large bowls, sprinkled with the remaining coriander.

Tip

To prepare mussels, scrub off any dirt and remove any barnacles. Remove the beard, if any, that sticks out between the shells. Discard any mussels that are already open or have a cracked shell.

St David's Day Leek and Mustard Potato Tart

Flavours and textures combined in a fittingly Welsh dish. Serve hot with seasonal steamed zero *POINTS* value vegetables or cold with a zero *POINTS* value spring salad.

Serves 4 | Takes 25 minutes to prepare, 30 minutes to cook | 9½ *POINTS* values per recipe
185 calories per serving | ⊙

450 g (1 lb) potatoes, peeled and cut into pieces
2 large leeks, washed and sliced finely
1 egg
150 ml (5 fl oz) skimmed milk

100 g (3½ oz) low fat soft cheese
1 tablespoon Dijon mustard
salt and freshly ground black pepper

1 Bring a pan of water to the boil, add the potatoes and cook until tender. At the same time, steam the leeks, preferably over the potatoes. Do this in a covered metal colander. When cooked, drain the potatoes well, season and mash. Set the leeks aside.

2 Preheat the oven to Gas Mark 7/220°C/fan oven 200°C. Line a 20 cm (8 inch) loose bottomed cake tin with non stick baking paper and then pile in the mashed potatoes and press down to make a base. Bake in the oven for 15 minutes until it has formed a crust.

3 Season the steamed leeks, pile on top of the potato base and spread to cover the tart base evenly.

4 In a jug, beat together the egg, milk, soft cheese and mustard and season. Pour over the leeks and return to the oven for a further 10–15 minutes, until the tart is set and golden. Serve either hot or cold.

Beef and Guinness Casserole

Casseroles are easy to make, yet so delicious to eat. Get stuck in for St Patrick's Day.

Serves 4 | Takes 15 minutes to prepare, 2 hours 10 minutes to cook | 21 *POINTS* values per recipe

345 calories per serving

low fat cooking spray

500 g (1 lb 2 oz) lean beef fillet steak, visible fat removed and cut into chunks

2 large onions, sliced

3 celery sticks, chopped

2 carrots, peeled and sliced

300 ml (10 fl oz) hot beef stock

600 ml (20 fl oz) Guinness

175 g (6 oz) mushrooms, sliced

2 teaspoons fresh parsley, chopped

1 teaspoon dried thyme

450 g (1 lb) potatoes, peeled and cut into chunks

salt and freshly ground black pepper

---

1 Preheat the oven to Gas Mark 4/180°C/fan oven 160°C.

2 Place a large, lidded, flameproof and ovenproof casserole dish over a high heat and spray with the cooking spray. Add the beef a handful at a time, so that it seals and browns. Add the onions, celery and carrots and cook over a medium heat for 3–4 minutes.

3 Add the stock, Guinness, mushrooms, parsley, thyme and seasoning. Bring up to the boil, then cover and transfer to the oven. Cook for 1½ hours.

4 Add the potatoes. Cover, return to the oven and cook for another 30 minutes, or until the potatoes are done and the meat is tender.

Tip

Use the same amount of stewing steak instead of fillet steak. Just make sure that it is very lean. The *POINTS* values will be 5 per serving.

Banana and Chocolate Muffins

NEW RECIPE

These yummy chocolate flecked muffins are a great way to use up any over-ripe speckled bananas that are left in the fruit bowl.

Makes 12 | Takes 10–12 minutes to prepare, 20 minutes to bake | 28 **POINTS** values per recipe
163 calories per recipe | Ⓥ | ✳

low fat cooking spray
225 g (8 oz) self raising flour
1 teaspoon bicarbonate of soda
100 g (3½ oz) caster sugar
15 g (½ oz) dark chocolate, grated finely

1 egg, beaten
150 g (5 oz) low fat vanilla yogurt
125 ml (4 fl oz) skimmed milk
2 ripe bananas, mashed
50 g (1¾ oz) low fat spread, melted

1. Preheat the oven to Gas Mark 6/200°C/fan oven 180°C and spray a 12 hole non stick muffin tin with the cooking spray.

2. Sift the flour and bicarbonate of soda into a mixing bowl, then stir in the sugar and grated chocolate.

3. Beat the egg with the yogurt and milk then add to the dry ingredients, followed by the mashed bananas and low fat spread. Stir just until mixed; the batter should still be slightly lumpy. Don't overmix or the muffins will turn out tough.

4. Spoon the muffin batter into the prepared tin and bake for 20 minutes until well risen and firm. Leave to stand for a couple of minutes then turn out and cool on a wire rack.

Lemon Meringue Pie

A low *POINTS* values version of a classic dessert, this is sure to be a crowd pleaser with its tangy filling and crisp meringue topping.

Serves 6 | Takes 20 minutes to prepare, 30 minutes to cook | 17 *POINTS* values per recipe
219 calories per serving | ♥

3 x 45 g (1½ oz) sheets filo pastry
low fat cooking spray
4 tablespoons cornflour

finely grated zest and juice of a lemon
150 g (5½ oz) caster sugar
2 eggs, separated

1 Preheat the oven to Gas Mark 4/180°C/fan oven 160°C. Cut each sheet of filo pastry in half to make two squares, then layer the squares on a 20 cm (8 inch) metal pie plate, spraying with the cooking spray between each layer. Scrunch the overhanging pastry up on to the rim of the pie plate. Place on a baking tray and bake for 10 minutes until crisp.

2 Meanwhile, place the cornflour in a non stick saucepan and add the lemon zest and juice. Stir to a smooth paste then add 40 g (1½ oz) of the sugar and 200 ml (7 fl oz) cold water. Heat, stirring constantly, until the mixture thickens, then simmer for 1 minute.

3 Remove the lemon mixture from the heat and mix in the egg yolks. Pour into the baked filo case and leave to cool and set for 5 minutes.

4 In a clean, grease free bowl, whisk the egg whites to stiff peaks. Gradually beat in the rest of the sugar until you have a stiff, glossy meringue. Spoon on top of the lemon filling, spreading right to the edges of the pastry case. Swirl the top of the meringue with the back of a spoon.

5 Bake the lemon meringue pie for 25–30 minutes until the meringue is crisp and golden. Serve slightly warm or at room temperature.

March

April

May

Easter Sunday Roast Lamb with Thyme and Mint Gravy

To cook this the Weight Watchers way, all the fat that would usually be left on the joint is removed. However, to prevent it from drying out, the joint is covered with a delicious herby, yogurt crust that keeps the meat succulent.

Serves 8 | Takes 15 minutes to prepare, 1 hour to cook + resting | 35 *POINTS* values per recipe
350 calories per serving

1.5 kg (3 lb 5 oz) leg of lamb, all visible fat removed
500 g (1 lb 2 oz) 0% fat Greek yogurt
1 teaspoon toasted cumin seeds, crushed in a pestle and mortar
a small bunch of mint, chopped

a small bunch of thyme, stems removed and leaves chopped
200 ml (7 fl oz) vegetable stock
salt and freshly ground black pepper

1   Preheat the oven to Gas Mark 5/190°C/fan oven 170°C. Rub the lamb all over with seasoning and place in a roasting tray.

2   Mix together the yogurt, cumin, mint and thyme and smear all over the meat, piling it up on the top. Roast the lamb for about 1 hour depending on how much the joint weighs (see Tip).

3   Remove the lamb from the oven. Wrap it in foil on a carving board and let it rest for 20 minutes before carving.

4   To make the gravy, place the roasting tin on the hob, using an oven glove to hold it, and heat. Add the stock and let it bubble for a few minutes while you scrape up all the baked on juices with a wooden or metal spatula. Strain the gravy through a sieve and into a serving jug. Serve three slices of lamb (100 g/3½ oz) per person, with the gravy.

Tip

On the bone joints of lamb, such as leg of lamb, need 20 minutes roasting time per 450 g (1 lb). Rolled joints of lamb, i.e. with no bone, need 25 minutes roasting time per 450 g (1 lb). Remove all visible fat from the joint and wrap in foil until the last 20 minutes when the foil should be removed to allow the joint to crisp.

Potato and Spinach Curry (Saag Aloo)

This is a classic Indian dish that is satisfying on its own or as an accompaniment to meat or fish.

Serves 4 | Takes 5 minutes to prepare, 50 minutes to cook | 10 *POINTS* values per recipe
220 calories per serving | ❤ | ❀

1 kg (2 lb 4 oz) fresh spinach, rinsed, drained and large stalks removed, or 500 g (1 lb 2 oz) frozen spinach
low fat cooking spray
2 teaspoons whole black mustard seeds
1 onion, sliced thinly
2 garlic cloves, chopped finely

900 g (2 lb) potatoes, peeled and cut into 2.5 cm (1 inch) cubes
½ teaspoon cayenne pepper or dried chilli flakes
1 teaspoon ground cumin
1 teaspoon ground coriander
salt and freshly ground black pepper

1   If using fresh spinach, put into a large, lidded, non stick pan with very little water and cook, covered, for 5 minutes until wilted. Season, drain and chop. Set aside.

2   Spray the same saucepan with the cooking spray, add the mustard seeds and cook for a couple of seconds until they pop, then add the onion and garlic and stir fry for 2 minutes.

3   Add the potatoes and cayenne pepper or chilli flakes and fry for another 2 minutes. Add the spinach, cumin, coriander and seasoning and 300 ml (½ pint) water. Bring to the boil, cover and simmer over the lowest possible heat for 30–40 minutes until the potatoes are tender. Stir occasionally, adding a little more water if the mixture looks like it might become too dry. Serve.

Tip

If using frozen spinach, omit step 1 and add directly to the pan in step 3.

Orecchiette with Pork Ragù

Fennel seeds and chilli are key flavouring ingredients in traditional Italian sausages, which are often used for rich pasta sauces like this one. Shaped pasta such as orecchiette, which literally translates as 'little ears', catches the meat sauce so that it doesn't fall to the bottom of your bowl.

Serves 4 | Takes 35 minutes | 27½ **POINTS** values per recipe | 393 calories per serving | ❄ (ragù sauce only)

500 g (1 lb 2 oz) extra lean pork mince
2 large garlic cloves, crushed
½ teaspoon fennel seeds
¼ teaspoon dried chilli flakes
1 tablespoon freshly chopped rosemary or
  1 teaspoon dried

500 g carton passata
225 g (8 oz) dried orecchiette (or any other pasta shape)
225 g (8 oz) broccoli, cut into small florets
50 g (1¾ oz) very low fat plain fromage frais
salt and freshly ground black pepper

1   In a large, lidded, non stick frying pan, dry fry the pork mince for 5 minutes, over a high heat, to brown. Add the garlic, fennel, chilli flakes and rosemary and cook for 1 minute.

2   Stir in the passata and seasoning, cover, and simmer for 30 minutes.

3   Bring a large pan of water to the boil and cook the pasta according to the packet instructions, adding the broccoli for the last 3 minutes of the cooking time. Drain, reserving 100 ml (3½ fl oz) of the cooking water.

4   Toss the pasta and broccoli with the sauce, and stir in the fromage frais and reserved cooking water. Serve immediately in deep, warmed bowls.

Cajun Fish Cakes

These spicy fish cakes are typical of the Creole cooking style developed in the southern USA. Serve with a salad of ripe tomatoes, red onions and fresh basil, dressed with lemon juice, for no additional *POINTS* values.

Serves 4 | Takes 35 minutes | 11 *POINTS* values per recipe | 169 calories per serving

300 g (10½ oz) large potatoes, peeled and chopped
1 teaspoon paprika
1 teaspoon cumin seeds
1 teaspoon mustard seeds

1 teaspoon dried oregano
1 teaspoon dried thyme
4 x 150 g (5½ oz) cod fillets
salt and freshly ground black pepper

1   Bring a pan of water to the boil and cook the potatoes for 20 minutes, until tender. Drain and mash.

2   Meanwhile, grind the spices, herbs and seasoning in a pestle and mortar or spice grinder. Place in a mixing bowl.

3   Preheat the grill to hot and line the grill pan with foil. Grill the cod for about 3 minutes or so on each side, then leave until cool enough to handle. Flake into the bowl of spices, discarding the skin and bones.

4   Add the mashed potatoes and mix together. Using wet hands, form into eight patties. Grill for 3–4 minutes on each side, until golden brown and crunchy on the top, then serve.

Spicy Pork and Pineapple Burgers

Homemade potato wedges are very easy to make, and create a great meal with these pork burgers. Serve with a crunchy zero *POINTS* value spring salad.

Serves 4 | Takes 15 minutes to prepare, 30 minutes to cook | 25½ *POINTS* values per recipe | 446 calories per serving

½ vegetable stock cube
4 x 250 g (9 oz) baking potatoes, unpeeled and each cut into 8 wedges
low fat cooking spray
500 g (1 lb 2 oz) lean pork mince

227 g can pineapple rings in juice, drained and chopped
40 g (1½ oz) fresh breadcrumbs
4 spring onions, chopped
2 tablespoons Thai sweet chilli sauce
salt and freshly ground black pepper

1 Preheat the oven to Gas Mark 7/220°C/fan oven 200°C and place a large baking tray in the oven to preheat.

2 Bring a pan of water to the boil, add the stock cube and potato wedges, bring back to the boil and simmer for 5 minutes.

3 Drain the potatoes well, return to the pan and shake around lightly to roughen the edges. Spray with the cooking spray and tip out on to the hot tray, shaking to distribute the wedges in a single layer. Cook in the oven for 30 minutes, turning halfway through.

4 Meanwhile, make the burgers by mixing together the pork mince, chopped pineapple, breadcrumbs, spring onions, chilli sauce and seasoning. Using wet hands, shape into 4 large, flat burgers.

5 Heat a non stick frying pan until hot, spray with the cooking spray and cook the burgers for 2 minutes on each side to brown. Transfer to another baking tray that has been sprayed with the cooking spray and cook for 10–12 minutes in the oven, above the potato wedges. The juices should run clear when the thickest part of the burger is pierced with a skewer or sharp knife.

6 Serve the burgers with the wedges on the side.

Variation

Try mixing 1 tablespoon of Thai sweet chilli sauce with 1 tablespoon of tomato ketchup to reduce the spiciness of the chillies. The *POINTS* values per serving will remain the same.

Chicken and Spring Vegetable Fricassee

Fresh spring vegetables and creamy chicken – a delightful light meal for a spring evening.

Serves 4 | Takes 30 minutes | 17 **POINTS** values per recipe | 335 calories per serving

4 x 150 g (5½ oz) skinless boneless chicken breasts
250 g (9 oz) low fat soft cheese with garlic and herbs
low fat cooking spray
2 garlic cloves, crushed
200 g (7 oz) baby carrots, scrubbed
200 g (7 oz) button onions
200 g (7 oz) baby turnips or baby sweetcorn, halved

425 ml (¾ pint) vegetable stock
½ cauliflower, sliced into small florets
½ head of broccoli, sliced into small florets
a small bunch of tarragon or parsley, tough stems removed and chopped (optional)
4 tablespoons virtually fat free fromage frais
salt and freshly ground black pepper

1   With a sharp knife, make a deep incision into the side of each chicken breast to make a pocket. Push a teaspoon of the soft cheese into each slit then season. Heat a lidded, flameproof casserole dish and spray with the cooking spray. Brown the chicken breasts on both sides and then remove to a plate.

2   Spray the pan again and add the garlic, carrots, onions and turnips or baby sweetcorn and brown them all over for 5 minutes.

3   Return the chicken to the casserole and add the stock. Bring to the boil, scraping up any stuck on juices from the bottom of the pan with a wooden spatula. Cover and simmer for 10 minutes.

4   Add the cauliflower, broccoli, tarragon or parsley, if using, and the remaining soft cheese. Season and cover, then simmer for a further 5–10 minutes, until the cauliflower is tender and the chicken is cooked through.

5   Allow to cool a little and then stir in the fromage frais and serve.

Citrus-Crusted Salmon

A whole side of salmon makes for an impressive-looking dish on a buffet, and with a delectable crisp crumb crust, this is positively mouth watering. The salmon can easily be prepared ahead, covered and stored in the fridge until ready to cook.

Serves 8 | Takes 8 minutes to prepare, 15 minutes to cook | 31 *POINTS* values per recipe | 217 calories per serving

750 g (1 lb 10 oz) salmon fillet
4 medium slices bread, torn
4 tablespoons freshly chopped coriander
25 g (1 oz) low fat spread, melted

zest and juice of a lemon
zest and juice of an orange
salt and freshly ground black pepper

1   Preheat the oven to Gas Mark 5/190°C/fan oven 170°C. Season the salmon and place on a foil lined baking tray.

2   Put the bread and coriander in a food processor and whizz until fine crumbs, then mix with the low fat spread, citrus zests and 4 tablespoons of the combined citrus juice. Drizzle the remaining juice over the salmon.

3   Press the crumb crust on to the salmon fillet then bake in the oven for 15 minutes until the crust is golden and crisp, and the salmon is cooked through. Transfer to a serving platter and serve hot.

Warm Chicken Salad with Lemon Dressing

You can buy so many delicious salad leaves these days, which give such great flavour to your salads.

Serves 4 | Takes 10 minutes to prepare, 15 minutes to cook | 14½ *POINTS* values per recipe | 195 calories per serving

4 x 150 g (5½ oz) skinless boneless chicken breasts
175 g (6 oz) fine green beans, trimmed
1 bag of rocket leaves (or watercress)
a large handful of young spinach leaves, rinsed
½ Iceberg lettuce, shredded
1 teaspoon finely grated lemon zest

1 tablespoon lemon juice
1 tablespoon white wine or rice vinegar
2 tablespoons olive oil
1 teaspoon Dijon mustard
salt and freshly ground black pepper

1 Preheat the grill to medium high and line the grill pan with foil. Grill the chicken breasts, turning once, until tender and cooked through; they will take about 15 minutes to cook.

2 Meanwhile, bring a pan of water to the boil and cook the green beans until just tender, about 4 minutes.

3 Rinse all the salad leaves and arrange in four serving bowls. Mix together the lemon zest and juice, vinegar, olive oil, mustard and seasoning.

4 Drain the green beans, then refresh them in cold water and drain well.

5 Slice the hot chicken and divide between the salads with the beans. Spoon the dressing over each portion, and serve at once.

Variation

Use a couple of bags of mixed salad leaves instead of the rocket, spinach and Iceberg lettuce, for the same *POINTS* values.

Honey and Sultana Drop Scones

A delicious tea time treat, these are also good for breakfast, especially as they can be made ahead of time and frozen very successfully. If you have two scones, the *POINTS* values will be 1½ per serving.

Makes 18 | Takes 15 minutes | 12 *POINTS* values per recipe | 42 calories per serving | 🅥 | ❄

125 g (4½ oz) self raising flour
1 egg
150 ml (5 fl oz) skimmed milk

4 rounded teaspoons clear honey
40 g (1½ oz) sultanas
low fat cooking spray

1 Sift the flour into a mixing bowl and make a well in the centre. Break the egg into the well then gradually beat in the milk until you have a smooth batter. Mix in the honey and sultanas.

2 Heat a non stick frying pan over a medium heat and spray with the cooking spray. Drop six separate tablespoonfuls of batter into the pan and cook for 1½ minutes until golden brown underneath and bubbly and almost set on top.

3 Flip and cook for 45–60 seconds on the other side. Transfer to a plate and keep warm, wrapped in a clean tea towel, while you cook the remaining batter in two more batches to make a total of 18 drop scones.

Chocolate, Rum and Raisin Pudding

Utterly delectable, this decadent hot chocolate pudding is wonderful served with a 60 g (2 oz) scoop of low fat vanilla ice cream, for an extra 1 *POINTS* value per serving.

Serves 2 | Takes 15 minutes to prepare + 1 hour soaking, 20–25 minutes to cook | 9 *POINTS* values per recipe
299 calories per serving |

25 g (1 oz) raisins
30 ml (1 fl oz) dark rum
2 tablespoons cocoa powder
25 g (1 oz) soft light brown sugar
200 ml (7 fl oz) skimmed milk

1 egg
½ teaspoon vanilla extract
2 slices wholemeal or white bread, diced into
2 cm (¾ inch) cubes, keep crusts on

1. Start this recipe an hour ahead by soaking the raisins in the rum until plump. When you are ready to make the pudding, preheat the oven to Gas Mark 4/180°C/fan oven 160°C.

2. Place the cocoa powder and sugar in a saucepan and gradually blend in the milk, then bring the mixture up to simmering point. Remove from the heat.

3. Whisk the egg and vanilla extract together in a bowl, then gradually pour in the warm chocolate milk, stirring all the time. Drain the raisins and add any rum that hasn't been absorbed by the raisins to the chocolate mixture.

4. Place half the bread and drained raisins in a baking dish and pour over half the chocolate custard, straining it through a sieve to remove any eggy threads. Repeat with the remaining ingredients and push the bread down into the chocolate mixture. Let it stand for 5 minutes for the bread to absorb the chocolate custard, and put the kettle on to boil.

5. Place the dish inside a roasting tin and pour enough boiling water around the dish to come about halfway up the sides. Bake in the oven on the centre shelf for 20–25 minutes – the pudding should be slightly risen and puffy, with a crisp top. Remove from the oven and allow it to stand for 5 minutes before serving.

March

April

May

Asparagus and Leek Tart

British asparagus is at its best in May, so make the most of it with this delicious seasonal tart.

Serves 2 | Takes 25 minutes | 8½ **POINTS** values per recipe | 204 calories per serving | Ⓥ | ❄

80 g (3 oz) puff pastry
1 large leek, chopped finely
1 tablespoon fresh thyme leaves
1 egg, beaten, for brushing

8 asparagus tips
a sprig of fresh rosemary
low fat cooking spray
salt and freshly ground black pepper

1 Preheat the oven to Gas Mark 6/200°C/fan oven 180°C.

2 Roll out the pastry into an 8 cm (3¼ inch) square and place it on a non stick baking sheet. Gently push up the edges of the pastry to make a slight ridge all the way round.

3 Fill a pan about a quarter full with water, bring to the boil and, using a steamer, steam the leek for 3 minutes until tender. If you do not have a steamer, cook the leek gently in simmering water. Drain, squeeze out any excess water and combine the leek with the thyme.

4 Brush the pastry square with some beaten egg to glaze and spoon the leek over the top, leaving a 1 cm (½ inch) gap around the edge.

5 Arrange the asparagus tips on top of the leek. Season well, place the rosemary on top and spray with the cooking spray. Bake for 15 minutes or until the pastry is cooked and golden.

Spicy Swedish Meatballs

This recipe is based on an original Swedish recipe for spicy meatballs with a sweet sauce. Serve with a zero **POINTS** value green vegetable, such as seasonal cooked, shredded cabbage.

Serves 4 | Takes 20 minutes to prepare, 15–20 minutes to cook | 20 **POINTS** values per recipe | 270 calories per serving

500 g (1 lb 2 oz) extra lean beef mince
1 small onion, chopped finely
2 garlic cloves, chopped finely
1½ tablespoons chopped fresh dill
1 egg, beaten

1 teaspoon Worcestershire sauce
2 tablespoons tomato purée
low fat cooking spray
2 tablespoons mango chutney
salt and freshly ground black pepper

1   Preheat the oven to Gas Mark 6/200°C/fan oven 180°C.

2   In a bowl, mix together the beef mince, onion, garlic, dill, egg, Worcestershire sauce, tomato purée and seasoning – this is easier to do with your hands, squeezing all the ingredients together. Shape the mince mixture into 12 small balls.

3   Spray a non stick frying pan with the cooking spray and gently brown the meatballs, turning occasionally to brown them all over. Remove the meatballs from the pan and place them in a casserole dish.

4   Add the mango chutney and 4 tablespoons of water to the frying pan and cook for 1 minute, stirring to gather all the bits from the pan.

5   Pour the mango sauce over the meatballs. Cover and cook in the oven for 15–20 minutes until cooked through.

6   Serve three meatballs per person with the sauce spooned over.

Lamb Koftas with Mint Dip

These lovely spring lamb kebabs are just perfect with the fresh herb dip.

Serves 8 | Takes 15 minutes to prepare, 10–15 minutes to cook | 27 **POINTS** values per recipe

145 calories per serving | ❋ (koftas only)

500 g (1 lb 2 oz) lean lamb mince
1 garlic clove, crushed
¼ teaspoon chilli powder
1 tablespoon chopped fresh coriander
1 tablespoon chopped fresh mint
1 egg, beaten
a dash of Tabasco sauce
25 g (1 oz) branflakes, crushed
1 teaspoon salt

For the dip
250 g tub Quark
a dash of Tabasco sauce
1 teaspoon lemon juice
1 teaspoon lime juice
1 teaspoon mint sauce or 1 tablespoon chopped fresh mint
grated zest of a lemon and a lime

1 Preheat the grill to medium high and line the grill pan with foil.

2 Mix together all the kofta ingredients, then divide into 8 equal portions. Using wet hands, form into long sausage shapes around 8 metal skewers or bamboo sticks.

3 Grill the kebabs for 10–15 minutes, turning frequently, until well-browned and thoroughly cooked.

4 Meanwhile, combine all the ingredients for the dip together until smooth and creamy.

5 Serve the koftas with the dip.

Tip

If using bamboo skewers, soak them in hot water for about 10 minutes before use, to prevent them from burning.

Variation

Try turkey mince instead of lamb. Serve with a garlic dip, made by omitting the mint, lime zest and juice and replacing them with a crushed garlic clove and some chopped fresh parsley, for 2 **POINTS** values per serving.

Chicken Laksa

A laksa is a Malaysian soupy noodle curry made with a dizzying array of ingredients.

Serves 4 | Takes 30 minutes | 15½ *POINTS* values per recipe | 260 calories per serving

low fat cooking spray

2 garlic cloves, crushed

2 teaspoons Thai red or green curry paste

400 g (14 oz) skinless boneless chicken breast fillets, cut into small pieces

3 tablespoons soy sauce

300 ml (10 fl oz) chicken stock

100 g (3½ oz) fine egg or rice noodles, broken up

1 teaspoon sugar

1 lemongrass stalk, chopped into 4 pieces and crushed slightly

5 kaffir lime leaves, rolled up and sliced finely crossways

2 tablespoons low fat coconut milk

To garnish

20 g (¾ oz) roasted peanuts, chopped

a small bunch of fresh coriander, chopped

1 Heat a non stick wok or large, non stick frying pan, spray with the cooking spray and fry the garlic until golden brown, adding a little water if necessary to prevent it from sticking. Add the curry paste and stir fry for 30 seconds.

2 Add the chicken pieces and stir briefly until thoroughly coated with the paste. Add the soy sauce, stock, noodles and sugar and cook for a further 2 minutes.

3 Add the lemongrass and lime leaves. Lower the heat and simmer for 10 minutes.

4 Remove the lemongrass pieces and stir in the coconut milk. Spoon into dishes to serve, garnished with the peanuts and coriander.

Tip

Thai curry paste is hot and spicy, so adjust the amount to your liking.

Mediterranean Baked Fish

Choose cod loin or haddock fillets to make this Mediterranean style fish dish – it's perfect for a special meal for two. Serve with lightly cooked fresh green seasonal zero *POINTS* value vegetables.

Serves 2 | Takes 10 minutes to prepare, 25 minutes to cook | 7 *POINTS* values per recipe | 391 calories per serving

low fat cooking spray

1 large red onion, thinly sliced

4 tomatoes, quartered

1 teaspoon dried mixed Italian herbs

2 rashers lean back bacon, trimmed of all fat

2 x 150 g (5½ oz) skinless cod loin or haddock fillets

2 level teaspoons tomato purée

1 teaspoon finely grated lemon zest

6 pitted black or green olives, in brine, sliced

9 large basil or flat leaf parsley leaves, reserving a few to garnish

salt and freshly ground black pepper

1   Preheat the oven to Gas Mark 5/190°C/170°C. Spray a roasting dish with the cooking spray and add the onion, tomatoes and mixed herbs.

2   Lay out the rashers of bacon on a board. Gently stretch them lengthwise and place a fish fillet at one end of each rasher. Spread the tomato purée over the fish, sprinkle with the lemon zest, olives and some of the basil or parsley leaves and roll up the bacon.

3   Place the bacon-wrapped fish on top of the onion and tomatoes and season. Cover with foil and bake for 20–25 minutes. Garnish with the remaining basil or parsley leaves and serve.

Spring Chicken Bake

Make the most of fresh, seasonal flavours in this simple spring chicken bake.

Serves 2 | Takes 15 minutes to prepare, 50 minutes to cook | 9 *POINTS* values per recipe | 337 calories per serving

250 g (9 oz) small new potatoes, scrubbed
250 g (9 oz) baby carrots, scrubbed
low fat cooking spray
2 whole sprigs of fresh rosemary, plus 1 sprig finely chopped
2 x 150 g (5½ oz) skinless boneless chicken breasts

50 g (1¾ oz) low fat soft cheese
1 garlic clove, crushed
finely grated zest of ½ a lemon
100 g (3½ oz) asparagus spears, trimmed
salt and freshly ground black pepper

1 Preheat the oven to Gas Mark 6/200°C/fan oven 180°C.

2 Put the potatoes and carrots into a roasting dish and spray with the cooking spray, turning to coat them. Add the whole rosemary sprigs and season. Transfer to the oven and roast for 15 minutes.

3 Meanwhile, use a sharp knife to cut a pocket into the thickest part of each chicken breast. Mix together the soft cheese, garlic, lemon zest and chopped rosemary. Pack this mixture into the pockets in the chicken breasts, close them up and secure with cocktail sticks.

4 Remove the roasting dish from the oven and position the chicken breasts on top. Spray with the cooking spray. Return to the oven and roast for a further 15 minutes.

5 Remove the roasting dish from the oven and arrange the asparagus spears in the roasting pan. Return to the oven for a further 15–20 minutes, or until the chicken is cooked. To check, insert a sharp knife into the thickest part of the chicken – the juices should run clear.

6 Serve the chicken with the roasted vegetables.

Variation

If you wish, use fresh thyme instead of rosemary.

Warm Spinach and Chick Pea Salad

A tasty and reviving salad that is great for lunch or as a light supper dish.

Serves 1 | Takes 8 minutes | 1½ **POINTS** values per recipe | 151 calories per serving | **Ⓥ**

low fat cooking spray
1 large garlic clove, chopped finely
1 teaspoon cumin seeds
75 g (2¾ oz) canned chick peas, drained and rinsed
200 g (7 oz) baby spinach leaves, stalks removed and washed

zest of ½ a lemon
3 teaspoons lemon juice
salt and freshly ground black pepper
½ medium red chilli, de-seeded and sliced thinly, to garnish

1 Heat a heavy based, non stick frying pan, spray with the cooking spray and fry the garlic, cumin seeds and chick peas for 2 minutes, stirring continuously. Add a little water if they start to stick and take care not to burn the garlic.

2 Stir in the spinach, lemon zest and juice and cook for another 2 minutes.

3 Season and serve immediately sprinkled with the fresh chilli.

Navarin of Lamb

A great Sunday lunch recipe, this makes the most of seasonal lamb and baby vegetables.

Serves 6 | Takes 15 minutes to prepare, 2½ hours to cook | 45½ *POINTS* values per recipe
314 calories per serving | ❋

750 g (1 lb 10 oz) lean lamb loin chops, cut into chunks
30 g (1¼ oz) flour, seasoned
low fat cooking spray
700 ml (25 fl oz) cold lamb or beef stock
2 tablespoons tomato purée
2 onions, chopped
450 g (1 lb) baby carrots, scrubbed

1 bouquet garni
18 sweet pickled small silverskin onions, drained and well rinsed
600 g (1 lb 5 oz) small new potatoes
150 g (5½ oz) fresh peas
2 tablespoons fresh chopped parsley, to garnish

1   Preheat the oven to Gas Mark 4/180°C/fan oven 160°C.

2   Roll the meat in the seasoned flour. Heat a large, lidded, flameproof and ovenproof casserole dish and spray with the cooking spray. Add the meat and brown on the hob. You may need to do this in batches.

3   Return all the meat to the pan. Mix any remaining flour into the stock with the tomato purée and pour it over the meat. Add the onions, carrots and bouquet garni and bring to the boil. Cover and cook in the oven for 1¼ hours.

4   Add the silverskin onions, potatoes and peas and cook for a further 45 minutes or until the vegetables are cooked. Remove the bouquet garni and serve sprinkled with the parsley.

Tip

If you don't have a pan that you can use both on the hob and in the oven, use a large frying pan and then transfer the meat to a casserole dish.

Lemon and Ginger Sponge Puddings

These steamed sponge puddings make the perfect finish to Sunday lunch and are served with a luscious lemon sauce.

Serves 4 | Takes 20 minutes to prepare, 25 minutes to cook | 22 *POINTS* values per recipe
284 calories per serving | **V** | ❋ (puddings only)

low fat cooking spray
4 thin slices lemon
60 g (2 oz) low fat spread
60 g (2 oz) caster sugar
zest and juice of a lemon
1 egg, beaten
100 g (3½ oz) wholemeal self raising flour, sifted

½ teaspoon baking powder
¼ teaspoon ground ginger
2 tablespoons skimmed milk
2 pieces stem ginger in syrup, drained and diced, plus 2 tablespoons ginger syrup
1 tablespoon cornflour
1 tablespoon clear honey

1 Lightly coat the inside of four mini pudding basins (150 ml/¼ pint) with the cooking spray. Place a lemon slice in the bottom of each basin. Cut 4 pieces of foil, each about 15 cm (6 inches) square and set aside with the prepared basins.

2 Using an electric whisk, cream the low fat spread, sugar and lemon zest together in a mixing bowl until pale and fluffy, then gradually beat in the egg.

3 Sift the flour, baking powder and ground ginger over the mixture and fold in with a large metal spoon. Next fold in the milk, stem ginger and 1 tablespoon of the lemon juice.

4 Divide the mixture between the pudding basins then cover each one with a square of foil, crimping it tightly under the lip of the basin. Place the puddings in a tiered steamer (see Tip), add boiling water to the base pan, cover tightly and steam for 25 minutes.

5 Meanwhile, blend the cornflour with the remaining lemon juice in a saucepan then add 200 ml (7 fl oz) cold water, followed by the ginger syrup and honey. When the puddings have cooked for 20 minutes, gradually bring the sauce to the boil, stirring frequently, until the sauce has thickened and become clear.

6 Unmould the sponge puddings with the aid of a small round knife and serve with the hot lemon sauce poured over.

Tip

If you don't have a steamer, these puddings can be cooked in the oven, although the result won't be quite as light. Preheat the oven to Gas Mark 4/180°C/fan oven 160°C. Place the covered pudding basins on a baking tray and bake for 15 minutes until risen and firm to the touch.

June

July

August

summer routine

Warm Broad Bean and Smoked Ham Pittas

This summery salad can be served as an accompaniment to fish or meat or stuffed into a pitta pocket as suggested in this recipe.

Serves 4 | Takes 10 minutes | 14½ **POINTS** values per recipe | 205 calories per serving

300 g (10½ oz) broad beans
low fat cooking spray
1 onion, sliced finely
1 red chilli, de-seeded and chopped finely
2 garlic cloves, crushed
1 tablespoon balsamic vinegar

50 g (1¾ oz) smoked ham, cut into small strips
a small bunch of mint, chopped
2 tablespoons virtually fat free fromage frais
salt and freshly ground black pepper
4 pitta breads, to serve

1 Bring a pan of water to the boil and cook the broad beans for about 5 minutes or until tender. Drain and slip from their skins, keeping the bright green beans.

2 Heat a non stick frying pan, spray with the cooking spray and stir fry the onion, chilli and garlic for a few minutes, until softened and golden.

3 Remove the pan from the heat and add the balsamic vinegar, ham, beans, mint, fromage frais and seasoning. Stir to mix.

4 Warm the pitta breads in the oven or toaster. Spoon the ham and bean mixture into the pittas and serve.

Sesame Beef Salad

NEW RECIPE

A warm salad that is full of contrasting flavours and textures.

Serves 1 | Takes 12 minutes | 4 *POINTS* values per recipe | 263 calories per serving

50 g (1¾ oz) crisp salad leaves

2 heaped tablespoons chopped fresh coriander

60 g (2 oz) mange tout, sliced thinly

low fat cooking spray

125 g (4½ oz) lean rump steak, trimmed of all fat and sliced thinly

1 heaped teaspoon sesame seeds

2 rounded teaspoons clear honey

juice of ½ a small lime

2 teaspoons soy sauce

1 Toss the salad leaves with the coriander and mange tout and pile onto a plate.

2 Heat a non stick frying pan until hot and spray with the cooking spray. Stir fry the steak for 2 minutes over a high heat until browned.

3 Sprinkle in the sesame seeds and stir fry for 30 seconds before adding the honey. Toss to mix, then add the lime juice and soy sauce. Bubble briefly, then spoon the steak and dressing over the salad. Serve immediately.

Risotto of Summer Vegetables

A creamy risotto with fresh vegetables – simple and delicious.

Serves 4 | Takes 55 minutes | 16 *POINTS* values per recipe | 279 calories per serving | Ⓥ

850 ml (1½ pints) vegetable stock
low fat cooking spray
4 large spring onions, chopped
250 g (9 oz) arborio (risotto) rice
1 courgette, sliced thinly
2 small carrots, peeled and cut into thin batons

125 g (4½ oz) fine asparagus, trimmed
  (halved if very long)
100 g (3½ oz) fresh peas
75 g (2¾ oz) low fat soft cheese
6 fresh chives, snipped, to garnish

1   Put the stock in a pan and bring to a simmer. Keep it covered on a low heat as you use it.

2   Heat a large wok or non stick frying pan and spray with the cooking spray. Gently fry the spring onions for 2 minutes. Add the rice and stir for a further 2 minutes until the rice becomes opaque.

3   Keeping the heat fairly low, add a couple of ladles of stock to the rice. Stir until the liquid is absorbed. The temperature will be right when you can just see a few bubbles rising to the surface, but not a vigorous boil.

4   Keep adding the stock, a couple of ladles at a time, stirring occasionally and always allowing it to be absorbed before adding more. After 10 minutes (you will have used about half the stock), add the courgette, carrots, asparagus and peas. Stir and continue adding the stock as before. After 25–30 minutes the rice should be tender with a rich, creamy consistency. If you run out of stock, use a little boiling water.

5   Stir in the low fat soft cheese and serve in warm bowls with the chives sprinkled on top.

Creamy Summery Pasta

This pasta recipe is full of early summer vegetables. Serve with steamed zero **POINTS** value vegetables of your choice, such as asparagus or baby courgettes.

Serves 4 | Takes 15 minutes | 24½ **POINTS** values per recipe | 470 calories per serving | 🟉

200 g (7 oz) fresh peas
350 g (12 oz) dried pasta shapes
low fat cooking spray
2 garlic cloves, sliced finely
a bunch of spring onions, sliced

200 g (7 oz) sugar snap peas
300 g (10½ oz) baby carrots, scrubbed and trimmed
200 g (7 oz) low fat soft cheese with garlic and herbs
a small bunch of fresh mint, chopped
salt and freshly ground black pepper

1 Bring a pan of water to the boil and cook the peas and pasta for 6–8 minutes or according to the packet instructions. Drain and replace in the pan.

2 Meanwhile, heat a wok or large, non stick frying pan and spray with the cooking spray. Stir fry the garlic over a medium heat until golden. Add all the remaining vegetables and continue to stir fry for a few minutes.

3 Add the soft cheese and mint to the vegetables and gently stir in, then heat through. Add the vegetable mixture to the pasta, toss together, season and serve.

Shrimp Pancakes with Garlic Prawns

Perfect for a lunch with friends or for eating al fresco on a warm summer evening.

Serves 4 | Takes 35 minutes + 30 minutes resting | 12½ *POINTS* values per recipe | 194 calories per serving

low fat cooking spray
6 spring onions, chopped finely, plus extra to garnish
100 g (3½ oz) self raising flour
a large pinch of chilli powder or dried chilli flakes
1 egg
250 ml (9 fl oz) skimmed milk
a small bunch of fresh dill, coriander or parsley, chopped finely

225 g (8 oz) small frozen prawns, defrosted and chopped finely
salt and freshly ground black pepper

For the prawn marinade

16 raw king prawns, peeled and heads removed
grated zest and juice of a lemon
4 garlic cloves, chopped finely or crushed

1 Place the king prawns in a bowl with the lemon zest and juice, along with the garlic and some seasoning to marinate.

2 Heat a non stick frying pan and spray with the cooking spray. Stir fry the spring onions for 2 minutes, until softened, adding a little water if necessary to prevent them from sticking.

3 In a large bowl, combine the flour, chilli and seasoning, then make a well in the middle and add the egg and milk. Gradually stir in until you have a thick batter.

4 Stir in the spring onions, herbs and chopped prawns – the batter should be like thick cream. Leave for 30 minutes.

5 Heat a large, non stick pan, spray with the cooking spray and drop in tablespoonfuls of the batter. Cook in batches of three or four (the batter should make 12 small pancakes). Cook each batch for a couple of minutes on each side. Keep the pancakes warm in a low oven while you cook the king prawns.

6 In the same frying pan or a wok, stir fry the king prawns and the marinade over a high heat for two minutes, until the prawns are cooked through.

7 Serve the prawns with the pancakes. Sprinkle with the extra chopped spring onion to garnish.

Lemon Thyme Chicken with Summer Vegetables

Lemon juice, lemon thyme and baby vegetables give chicken breasts a delicious summery flavour. Serve with 150 g (5½ oz) cooked new potatoes per person, for an extra 1½ *POINTS* values per serving.

Serves 4 | Takes 15 minutes to prepare, 30 minutes to cook | 10½ *POINTS* values per recipe | 206 calories per serving

low fat cooking spray

4 x 150 g (5½ oz) boneless skinless chicken breasts

300 ml (10 fl oz) chicken stock

juice of a lemon

5 spring onions or 200 g (7 oz) baby leeks, trimmed

125 g (4½ oz) baby sweetcorn

150 g (5½ oz) fine green beans, mange tout or sugar snap peas

8 baby carrots, scrubbed and halved or 1 large carrot, peeled and cut into fine strips

1 tablespoon fresh chopped parsley

4 sprigs fresh thyme (lemon thyme, if possible)

1 level tablespoon cornflour blended with a little cold water

salt and freshly ground black pepper

To garnish

1 sprig fresh thyme or parsley

lemon wedges

1   Heat a large, lidded, non stick frying pan and spray with the cooking spray. Add the chicken breasts and cook for 3–4 minutes on each side until browned.

2   Add the stock, lemon juice, spring onions or leeks, sweetcorn, green beans, mange tout or sugar snap peas, carrots, chopped parsley and thyme sprigs.

3   Simmer, partially covered, for 25–30 minutes or until the chicken is tender. Season.

4   Using a draining spoon, lift the chicken and vegetables onto warmed serving plates. Add the blended cornflour to the cooking liquid and stir until smooth and thickened. Pour over the chicken and serve, garnished with thyme or parsley and lemon wedges.

Butterflied Tandoori Chicken

The ideal summer chicken dish. Serve with a zero *POINTS* value seasonal green salad.

Serves 6 | Takes 20 minutes to prepare + marinating, 1 hour 20 minutes to cook | 40½ *POINTS* values per recipe
252 calories per serving

1.5 kg (3 lb 5 oz) chicken
300 ml (10 fl oz) low fat natural yogurt
3 garlic cloves, crushed
2.5 cm (1 inch) piece of fresh root ginger, peeled and chopped finely
1 tablespoon tandoori curry paste
1 teaspoon garam masala

salt and freshly ground black pepper

To garnish
a small bunch of fresh coriander, chopped (optional)
2 limes, cut into wedges

1 Remove the back bone and ribs from the chicken, turn the chicken so it is skin side up and press down firmly on the breastbone with the heel of your hand to flatten it out.

2 Remove all the skin, wash the bird under cold running water and then pat dry with kitchen paper.

3 To make the marinade, combine all of the remaining ingredients, except the garnish, in a bowl and then rub all over the chicken both inside and out. Cover and leave to marinate in the fridge for at least 1 hour and preferably overnight.

4 Preheat the oven to Gas Mark 6/200°C/fan oven 180°C and thread two 10 cm (4 inch) metal skewers in a criss-cross fashion through the chicken to keep it flat. Arrange the chicken on a wire rack in a roasting tin, spread with some of the marinade and roast for 40 minutes.

5 Turn the chicken over, spread with more of the marinade and roast for a further 40 minutes until each side is golden brown and cooked through. Leave to rest for a few minutes and then remove the skewers. Scatter with the fresh coriander, if using, and garnish with lime wedges.

Tip

To remove the back bone and ribs of a chicken, use poultry shears or tough kitchen scissors. Cut the chicken along the back and down each side of the back bone. Remove the back bone and discard. Snip the wishbone in half and open out the chicken, then snip out the ribs.

Carrot Cake Traybake

These lovely moist carrot cake slices are topped with a soft, creamy icing, dusted with mixed spice.

Makes 14 slices | Takes 15 minutes to prepare, 30 minutes to cook | 27½ *POINTS* values per recipe
133 calories per recipe | ⓥ | ❄

low fat cooking spray
3 eggs
125 g (4½ oz) caster sugar
75 g (2¾ oz) low fat spread, melted
150 g (5½ oz) self raising flour
1 heaped teaspoon mixed spice, plus a pinch to dust

250 g (9 oz) carrots, peeled and coursely grated

For the icing
100 g (3½ oz) low fat soft cheese
75 g (2¾ oz) 0% fat Greek yogurt
1 tablespoon icing sugar, sifted

1 Preheat the oven to Gas Mark 4/180°C/fan oven 160°C. Line a 17 x 25 cm (6½ x 10 inches) rectangular cake tin with non stick baking parchment and spray with the cooking spray.

2 In a large mixing bowl and using an electric whisk, beat the eggs and sugar for 3–4 minutes until the mixture is pale and thick, similar to the texture of lightly whipped cream. Pour in the low fat spread.

3 Sift the flour and 1 heaped teaspoon mixed spice into the bowl, then fold everything together until you have a smooth batter.

4 Stir in the carrots then pour the batter into the prepared tin. Bake for 25–30 minutes until the cake is firm and golden brown.

5 Remove from the oven and stand the tin on a wire rack while the cake cools.

6 Meanwhile, beat the soft cheese, yogurt and icing sugar together. When the cake is completely cool, remove from the tin and spread with the icing. Dust with a pinch of mixed spice and cut into 14 slices.

Creamy Gooseberry Fool

The creaminess of the Quark takes away any tartness from the gooseberies, creating a delicious summer fool.

Serves 6 | Takes 20 minutes + cooling + chilling | 16½ *POINTS* values per recipe
219 calories per serving | 🌱

450 g (1 lb) gooseberries, topped and tailed
2 tablespoons artificial sweetener
6 egg yolks

450 ml (16 fl oz) skimmed milk
2 x 250 g tubs Quark

1 Place the gooseberries in a lidded pan with 2 tablespoons of water, cover and bring to the boil. Reduce the heat and simmer for 5 minutes until pulpy. Stir in the artificial sweetener. Set aside to cool slightly.

2 Place the egg yolks in a bowl and beat. Put the milk in a saucepan and heat gently to just below boiling point. Remove the milk from the heat and pour it over the eggs, whisking to combine. Return the mixture to the pan and bring to the boil, stirring continuously until thickened.

3 Combine the custard, gooseberries and Quark, adding extra sweetener if required. Spoon into serving glasses, cool and then chill.

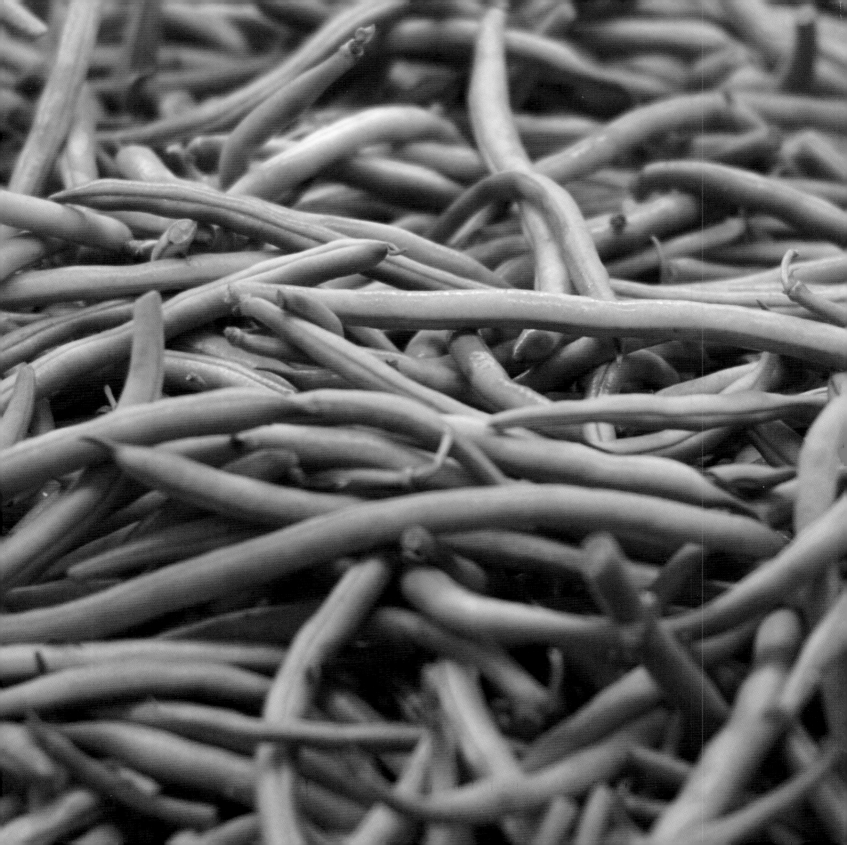

Summer

June
July
August

Blueberry Hotcakes

A luxurious American diner style breakfast or brunch.

Serves 4 | Takes 20 minutes | 14 *POINTS* values per recipe | 240 calories per serving | ⓥ | ❋ (hotcakes only)

150 g (5½ oz) self raising flour
a pinch of salt
2 teaspoons caster sugar
1 egg, separated, plus 1 egg white
200 ml (7 fl oz) skimmed milk
low fat cooking spray

175 g (6 oz) fresh blueberries

To serve
200 g pot very low fat fromage frais
4 teaspoons maple syrup or golden syrup

1   Sift the flour and salt into a mixing bowl. Stir in the sugar and make a well in the centre. Add the egg yolk and gradually whisk in the milk to give a thick batter.

2   In a separate clean bowl, whisk the egg whites to soft peaks then fold into the batter. Pour the batter into a measuring jug for easy pouring.

3   Heat a medium, non stick frying pan and spray with the cooking spray. Pour a quarter of the batter into the pan and swirl to cover the base evenly. Scatter with a small handful of blueberries (about 20 g/¾ oz). Cook over a medium heat for 2 minutes until the top is bubbly and almost set. Use a fish slice to flip the hotcake and cook for 1–1½ minutes until the second side is golden brown.

4   Remove from the pan and keep warm while you cook the remaining three hotcakes, wiping the pan out with kitchen paper and respraying with the cooking spray between each one.

5   Serve the warm blueberry hotcakes topped with fromage frais, the rest of the blueberries and syrup.

Garden Herb Soup

If you have an abundance of herbs in your garden, use them to full advantage in this delicious soup, which you can serve chilled or hot.

Serves 4 | Takes 10 minutes to prepare, 15 minutes to cook | 6½ *POINTS* values per recipe
112 calories per serving | ♥

2 teaspoons low fat spread
5 spring onions, finely chopped
6 tablespoons fresh herbs, such as parsley, chives, basil and oregano
600 ml (20 fl oz) vegetable stock

300 ml (10 fl oz) skimmed milk
175 g (6 oz) low fat soft cheese
1 level tablespoon cornflour, blended with 2 tablespoons cold water
salt and freshly ground black pepper

1 Melt the low fat spread in a large, non stick saucepan and sauté the spring onions until softened.

2 Add the herbs and stock, bring up to the boil, then reduce the heat and simmer for about 10 minutes.

3 Add the milk and soft cheese and heat, stirring until smooth. Stir in the blended cornflour and cook gently until thickened. Season to taste.

4 Serve immediately, or cool and chill until very cold for an iced summer soup.

Summer Stew with Gremolata

Gremolata is an Italian condiment, traditionally made with garlic, lemon zest and parsley. Here, breadcrumbs are added to provide an extra crunch.

Serves 4 | Takes 40 minutes | 8½ *POINTS* values per recipe | 207 calories per serving | Ⓥ | ❄

low fat cooking spray
350 g (12 oz) baby onions, peeled
250 g (9 oz) baby turnips, peeled
300 g (10½ oz) baby carrots, scrubbed and trimmed
2 garlic cloves, chopped finely
1 teaspoon dried mixed herbs
2 bay leaves
150 ml (5 fl oz) dry white wine
250 ml (9 fl oz) vegetable stock
275 g (9½ oz) baby courgettes

175 g (6 oz) fresh peas
salt and freshly ground black pepper

For the gremolata
2 slices white bread, about 75 g (2¾ oz), crusts removed
1 tablespoon olive oil
1 garlic clove, chopped finely
zest and juice of a lemon
1 tablespoon chopped fresh flat leaf parsley

1 Heat a large, lidded, heavy based saucepan and spray with the cooking spray. Add the onions and sauté, covered, for 4 minutes until they start to brown. Add the turnips, carrots, garlic, herbs and bay leaves and continue to cook, covered, for 3 minutes, stirring occasionally.

2 Pour in the wine and bring to the boil then cook until the wine has almost evaporated and the smell of alcohol has disappeared. Pour in the stock and simmer, uncovered, for 10 minutes, stirring occasionally.

3 Cover the pan and cook for another 5 minutes, then add the courgettes, peas and seasoning. Cook for a final 5 minutes.

4 While the vegetables are cooking, put the bread into a food processor and process until it forms breadcrumbs. Heat the oil in a frying pan and fry the breadcrumbs for 2 minutes until crisp and golden. Add the garlic and fry for another 30 seconds. Next, stir in the lemon zest and juice and the parsley.

5 Divide the vegetables between four plates and sprinkle with the gremolata.

Chicken Couscous Salad

A fast simple salad that can easily be packed in a lunch box or taken on a picnic.

Serves 2 | Takes 15 minutes + chilling | 10 **POINTS** values per recipe | 277 calories per serving

150 ml (5 fl oz) hot chicken stock
100 g (3½ oz) couscous
zest and juice of ½ a lemon
2 tablespoons fresh chopped coriander
1 peach, stoned and chopped
8 cherry tomatoes, halved

4 spring onions, chopped
½ green or yellow pepper, de-seeded and diced
175 g (6 oz) skinless, ready cooked chicken breast, sliced into bite size pieces
salt and freshly ground black pepper

1   In a large bowl, pour the hot chicken stock over the couscous, stir in the lemon zest and juice and 1 tablespoon of the coriander. Cover with clingfilm and leave to stand for 5 minutes.

2   Fluff up the couscous with a fork, transfer to a serving dish and leave to cool completely.

3   When cool, stir in the chopped peach, tomatoes, spring onions and pepper and check the seasoning. Stir in the chicken (or pop it on top of the salad) and then scatter the remaining coriander over it.

4   Chill until ready to use or transfer to a lunchbox and keep cool.

Ⓥ Variation

For a vegetarian option, you could use the same weight of cooked Quorn pieces instead of the chicken. The **POINTS** values per serving will be 4.

Thai Style Crab Cakes with Gingered Cucumber

An appetising light starter that can easily be prepared ahead (see Tip). However, don't mix the cucumber ribbons with the dressing until you are ready to serve, or they will lose their crunch.

Serves 6 | Takes 25 minutes | 9 *POINTS* values per recipe | 104 calories per serving | ❄ (crab cakes only)

finely grated zest and juice of a lime
1 red chilli, de-seeded and diced
1 lemongrass stalk, sliced
4 spring onions, sliced
4 heaped tablespoons chopped fresh coriander
400 g (14 oz) skinned haddock fillet, chopped roughly
170 g can white crab, drained
1 tablespoon cornflour

low fat cooking spray

For the gingered cucumber
1 large cucumber
1 tablespoon soy sauce
2 rounded teaspoons clear honey
1 teaspoon grated root ginger

1   Place the lime zest and half the lime juice in a food processor with half the chilli, lemongrass, spring onions and coriander. Whizz until finely chopped. Add the haddock and pulse until blended but not over processed. Add the crab and cornflour and mix again briefly.

2   Using damp hands so that the mixture doesn't stick, shape into 18 crab cakes, each around 5–6 cm (2–2½ inches) in diameter. Heat a non stick frying pan until hot and spray with the cooking spray. Fry the crab cakes for 2 minutes on each side until browned and cooked through.

3   For the gingered cucumber, using a vegetable peeler, shave the cucumber into ribbons. Make the dressing by mixing together the soy, honey and the rest of the lime juice. Squeeze the juice from the grated ginger into the dressing and discard the pulp. Stir in the remaining chilli. Toss the cucumber ribbons in the dressing just before serving with the crab cakes.

Tip

These aromatic crab cakes can be made and cooked in advance. Cool and store in the fridge then reheat in a single layer on a baking tray, covered with foil, for 10 minutes in an oven preheated to Gas Mark 4/180°C/fan oven 160°C.

Spare Ribs

Use your fingers (and plenty of napkins) to eat these delicious spare ribs.

Serves 2 | Takes 20 minutes to prepare, 50 minutes to cook | 14½ *POINTS* values per recipe | 400 calories per serving

350 g (12 oz) lean pork spare ribs
½ tablespoon honey
1 tablespoon tomato purée
1 tablespoon lemon juice
1½ tablespoons soy sauce
1½ tablespoons oyster sauce
½ teaspoon Chinese 5 spice powder

½ teaspoon hot chilli sauce (optional)
salt and freshly ground black pepper

To serve
2 spring onions, sliced finely
2 tomatoes, quartered

1   Preheat the oven to Gas Mark 6/200°C/fan oven 180°C. Put the spare ribs in a roasting pan.

2   In a small bowl, mix together the honey, tomato purée, lemon juice, soy sauce, oyster sauce, Chinese 5 spice powder and chilli sauce, if using. Season and then pour the sauce over the ribs, brushing them with a pastry brush to ensure they are well coated.

3   Roast for 40–50 minutes until tender, turning and brushing half way through.

4   Serve sprinkled with the spring onions and garnished with the tomatoes.

Tip

If you are using a barbecue for other food, put the ribs on the barbecue rack for the last 10 minutes of their cooking time for a delicious crispy finish.

Minty Lamb Burgers

Cook these on the barbecue and make the most of summer days.

Serves 2 | Takes 20 minutes + chilling | 10½ *POINTS* values per recipe | 246 calories per serving | ❄

225 g (8 oz) lean lamb mince
1 small onion, quartered
1 garlic clove
10 mint leaves
salt and freshly ground black pepper

To serve
60 g (2 oz) fresh salsa
a selection of zero *POINTS* value seasonal salad vegetables

1 Put the lamb, onion, garlic and mint in a food processor with a little seasoning and blend until it all comes together as a ball. (If you don't have a food processor, chop everything as finely as possible then use your hands to squeeze it together.)

2 Using wet hands, shape the meat into four burgers, place them on a plate and leave to chill in the fridge for at least an hour.

3 Preheat the grill to a medium heat or ensure your barbecue is ready. Cook the burgers for 5 minutes on each side or until cooked through.

4 Serve the burgers with the salsa and your choice of zero *POINTS* value seasonal salad vegetables.

Tip
Like your burgers a bit spicy? Omit the mint and use 1 tablespoon of chopped coriander, ½ a small de-seeded chilli and 1 teaspoon of ground cumin. The *POINTS* values will remain the same.

Smoked Mackerel and Potato Salad

This is a really tasty, filling salad.

Serves 2 | Takes 20 minutes | 14 *POINTS* values per recipe | 424 calories per serving

¼ Iceberg lettuce, shredded
a 'pea' sized blob of wasabi paste
4 tablespoons low fat natural yogurt
200 g (7 oz) small new potatoes, cooked
150 g (5½ oz) peppered mackerel, flaked into pieces
150 g (5½ oz) cherry tomatoes, halved

½ yellow pepper, de-seeded and chopped into small chunks
5 spring onions, chopped
1 celery stick, chopped
10 olives in brine, drained
2 lemon quarters, to garnish

1   Divide the lettuce between two large plates. To make the dressing, mix the wasabi and yogurt together in a small bowl or ramekin. Ensure it is mixed thoroughly and that the wasabi is evenly distributed. Taste the dressing and, if you like an even hotter flavour, add a little more wasabi.

2   Put the rest of the ingredients except the lemon quarters in a large mixing bowl and toss together. Divide the salad between the plates of lettuce and then top with the lemon quarters. You can serve the dressing over the top of the salad, or on the side. Serve immediately or, if you are taking this as a lunchbox salad, mix the lettuce into the salad, toss in the dressing and keep chilled in a suitable container.

Tip

Wasabi is a Japanese horseradish sold in a tube. It's available in most large supermarkets with the Oriental ingredients. If you prefer to use British horseradish, use a level tablespoon or to taste.

Variation

Some supermarkets sell ready cooked, cold, smoked trout fillets, which would also work well in this recipe.

Pastrami and Ricotta Pasta

A delicious light summery pasta dish.

Serves 2 | Takes 25 minutes | 9½ **POINTS** values per recipe | 250 calories per serving

80 g (3 oz) dried fusilli pasta
75 g (2¾ oz) ricotta cheese
10 pitted black olives in brine, sliced
50 g (1¾ oz) cherry tomatoes, halved

4 x 10 g (¼ oz) slices of pastrami, chopped roughly
50 g bag of wild rocket, chopped
salt and freshly ground black pepper

1   Bring a pan of water to the boil and cook the pasta for 12–15 minutes or according to the packet instructions until 'al dente'. Drain and rinse in cold water until cold. Empty into a bowl.

2   Stir through the ricotta, olives, tomatoes, pastrami and rocket. Check the seasoning and serve.

Ⓥ Variation

Replace the pastrami with the same quantity of vegetarian ham, for 4½ **POINTS** values per serving.

Easy Apricot Scones

These fruity scones are delicious split and spread with 2 teaspoons low fat soft cheese per scone, for an additional ½ *POINTS* value per serving.

Makes 12 scones | Takes 10 minutes to prepare, 15 minutes to cook | 17 *POINTS* values per recipe
93 calories per scone | ❤ | ❄ recommended

225 g (9 oz) self raising flour
a pinch of salt
25 g (1 oz) low fat spread
25 g (1 oz) caster sugar

50 g (1¾ oz) ready to eat dried apricots, diced
150 g (5 fl oz) low fat natural yogurt
low fat cooking spray
2 teaspoons skimmed milk

1 Preheat the oven to Gas Mark 6/200°C/fan oven 180°C. Reserve 2 teaspoons of the flour for rolling out, then sift the rest into a mixing bowl with a pinch of salt. Rub in the low fat spread until the mixture looks like breadcrumbs then stir in the sugar and apricots.

2 Add the yogurt to the bowl and mix to bind together until you have a soft but not sticky dough. Add a few drops of water if needed.

3 Dust the work surface with the reserved flour than pat or roll the scone dough to a thickness of 2 cm (¾ inch). Using a 5 cm (2 inch) cutter, stamp out 12 scones, re-rolling as needed. Place on a baking tray sprayed with the cooking spray.

4 Brush the tops of the scones with the milk then bake in the oven for 12–15 minutes until risen, firm and golden. Cool slightly on a wire rack before eating.

Variation

Try making some classic fruit scones by replacing the apricots with 50 g (1¾ oz) sultanas, for the same *POINTS* values per scone. If you leave out the dried fruit altogether for plain sweet scones, the *POINTS* values remain the same.

June

July

August

Quick Chorizo and Bean Chilli

A supremely quick and easy chilli made with store cupboard ingredients and fresh tomatoes and herbs.

Serves 4 | Takes 10 minutes to prepare, 10 minutes to cook | 29½ *POINTS* values per recipe | 214 calories per serving

400 g (14 oz) cherry tomatoes, de-seeded
1 tablespoon dried mixed herbs
400 g can kidney beans, drained
400 g can butter beans, drained

1 red chilli, de-seeded and finely chopped
150 g (5½ oz) chorizo sausage, thinly sliced, each slice
  cut in half
1 tablespoon fresh coriander, chopped

1   Place the cherry tomatoes in a blender with the mixed herbs and whizz to make a sauce.

2   Transfer the tomato sauce to a lidded, non stick saucepan and add the kidney and butter beans, chilli and 100 ml (3½ fl oz) water. Bring to the boil, cover and simmer for 10 minutes, then add the chorizo and heat through.

3   Add the coriander and serve.

Orange and Basil Chicken

This is an excellent dish for serving to a large group of people as it's so quick to prepare and easy to cook. The tangy orange sauce glazes the chicken and keeps it really moist.

Serves 8 | Takes 5 minutes to prepare, 20 minutes to cook | 21½ **POINTS** values per recipe | 176 calories per serving

125 g (4½ oz) marmalade
juice of 2 oranges
juice of 2 lemons

3 tablespoons freshly chopped basil
8 x 125 g (4½ oz) skinless boneless chicken breasts
salt and freshly ground black pepper

1   Preheat the oven to Gas Mark 6/200°C/fan oven 180°C. Blend the marmalade with the citrus juices, basil and seasoning, then pour over the chicken breasts in an ovenproof dish.

2   Place the dish in the oven and cook for 20 minutes or until cooked through, basting the chicken with the sauce half way through. Serve on warmed plates.

Aubergine Parmigiana

This tasty recipe exudes the flavours of the Mediterranean.

Serves 2 | Takes 30 minutes to prepare, 25 minutes to cook | 10 *POINTS* values per recipe
230 calories per serving | Ⓥ

1 yellow pepper, de-seeded and quartered
1 large courgette, cut into 1 cm (½ inch) slices
low fat cooking spray
1 aubergine, cut into 1 cm (½ inch) slices
400 g can chopped tomatoes

zest of a lemon
1 tablespoon shredded fresh basil
125 g light mozzarella, sliced thinly
15 g (½ oz) Parmesan cheese, freshly grated
salt and freshly ground black pepper

1 Preheat the grill to its highest setting and place the pepper and courgette slices on the grill tray. Lightly mist with the cooking spray and place under the grill. Grill the courgette slices for 5 minutes on each side until golden. Grill the peppers for 8–10 minutes until the skins are charred.

2 Transfer the courgettes to a plate. Place the peppers in a bowl, cover and leave to cool, then peel off the skins.

3 Place the aubergine slices on the grill pan, mist with the cooking spray and grill for 3–4 minutes on each side until browned.

4 Meanwhile, preheat the oven to Gas Mark 6/200°C/fan oven 180°C. Make the tomato sauce by simmering the tomatoes, lemon zest, basil and seasoning for 6–8 minutes until slightly thickened.

5 Spread half the tomato sauce in the base of a small baking dish and lay half of the aubergines on top. Cover with the courgettes and peppers, add the remaining aubergines and tomato sauce, followed by the sliced mozzarella and grated Parmesan. Bake for 20–25 minutes until bubbling.

Sunshine Spaghetti

NEW RECIPE

Sun ripened tomatoes, olives, garlic and peppers burst with flavours redolent of the Mediterranean in this simple recipe.

Serves 2 | Takes 15 minutes | **7 *POINTS*** values per recipe | 333 calories per serving | Ⓥ

125 g (4½ oz) dried spaghetti
low fat cooking spray
1 yellow or orange pepper, de-seeded and diced
a pinch of crushed dried chillies
2 garlic cloves, crushed

400 g can cherry tomatoes
40 g (1½ oz) pitted black olives in brine, drained and chopped roughly
1 teaspoon caster sugar

1 Bring a pan of water to the boil and cook the spaghetti according to the packet instructions until al dente.

2 Meanwhile, heat a non stick saucepan until hot and spray with the cooking spray. Add the pepper and cook for 3–4 minutes until starting to brown at the edges. Add the chillies and garlic and cook for 1 minute.

3 Stir in the tomatoes, olives and sugar, then simmer briskly for 5 minutes until the sauce is slightly reduced. Drain the pasta then toss with the sauce and serve in warm bowls.

Rosemary Redcurrant Lamb

When you need something special for a cosy, intimate dinner for two, try this recipe as it looks stunning and tastes divine. Serve on a bed of freshly cooked zero **POINTS** value seasonal vegetables.

Serves 2 | Takes 15 minutes to prepare, 25–35 minutes to cook | 13 **POINTS** values per recipe
330 calories per serving | ❄

2 x 125 g (4½ oz) lamb loins
25 g (1 oz) fresh white breadcrumbs
2 tablespoons redcurrant jelly
1 teaspoon finely chopped fresh rosemary

2 thin cut streaky bacon rashers
1 teaspoon olive oil
salt and freshly ground black pepper

1   Preheat the oven to Gas Mark 5/190°C/fan oven 170°C.

2   Make a 2.5 cm (1 inch) slit along the top of each lamb loin – the slit should be fairly deep.

3   Mix together the breadcrumbs, redcurrant jelly and rosemary and then spread this mixture into the slit in each lamb loin.

4   Stretch and flatten each bacon rasher with the back of a knife. Now wrap a stretched rasher around each loin – this helps to keep the filling in.

5   Brush each lamb parcel with a little olive oil and then season. Roast for 25 minutes if you like your lamb slightly pink, or 35 minutes if you prefer your lamb well cooked. Serve.

Tip

When presenting this dish, slice the cooked lamb into thin rings cut slightly on a slant.

Mexican Tortillas with Spicy Beef

Spicy beef, fresh salsa and lettuce and soft tortillas – tasty and great fun for all the family.

Serves 4 | Takes 50 minutes | 28 **POINTS** values per recipe | 462 calories per serving

low fat cooking spray
2 onions, chopped
2 garlic cloves, crushed
300 g (10½ oz) extra lean beef mince
400 g can chopped tomatoes
½–1 teaspoon dried chilli flakes
1 tablespoon Worcestershire or soy sauce
½ teaspoon sugar
100 ml (3½ fl oz) white wine
300 ml (10 fl oz) vegetable stock
salt and freshly ground black pepper

For the salsa
6 plum tomatoes, quartered, de-seeded and chopped finely
1 small red onion, chopped finely
1 small red chilli, de-seeded and chopped finely
a small bunch of fresh coriander, chopped
juice of a lime
2 teaspoons balsamic vinegar

To serve
8 medium flour tortillas
½ Iceberg lettuce, shredded

1   To make the salsa, mix all the salsa ingredients together in a small, non metallic bowl and chill until needed.

2   Heat a large, non stick frying pan, spray with the cooking spray and then stir fry the onions and garlic for 5 minutes, or until softened, adding a little water if they start to stick.

3   Add the beef and stir fry until browned all over. Add the chopped tomatoes, chilli, Worcestershire or soy sauce, sugar, wine, stock and seasoning. Bring to the boil and then simmer for 20 minutes.

4   Meanwhile, heat the tortillas as instructed on the packet.

5   To serve, fill the tortillas with the spicy beef, shredded lettuce and salsa. Alternatively, place all the components in different serving plates and bowls and let diners make their own.

Chinese Chicken

Serve this dish with egg fried rice, made with 145 g (5¼ oz) cooked cold brown rice and 3 finely chopped spring onions, heated thoroughly for 2 minutes before adding 1 lightly beaten egg and 75 g (2¾ oz) petit pois. Cook, stirring to break up the egg, for an extra 1½ **POINTS** values per serving.

Serves 4 | Takes 30 minutes | 9½ **POINTS** values per recipe | 205 calories per serving

4 x 150 g (5½ oz) skinless boneless chicken breasts, cut into small chunks
1 garlic clove, crushed
2.5 cm (1 inch) piece of fresh root ginger, peeled and grated
2 tablespoons soy sauce
juice of ½ a lemon
low fat cooking spray

1 green pepper, de-seeded and sliced
1 carrot, peeled and sliced finely
½ red chilli, de-seeded and sliced finely
1 onion, sliced
100 ml (3½ fl oz) white wine vinegar
2 tablespoons granulated artificial sweetener
100 ml (3½ fl oz) passata
2 spring onions, sliced finely

1 Put the chicken chunks in a non metallic bowl and mix with the garlic, ginger, 1 tablespoon soy sauce and lemon juice.

2 Heat a wok until hot. Spray with the cooking spray and stir fry the chicken for 5 minutes until starting to brown. Add the pepper, carrot, chilli and onion and stir fry for a further 3 minutes.

3 Add the vinegar, sweetener, passata and remaining soy sauce. Cook for 2 minutes until starting to thicken. Sprinkle over the spring onions and serve.

Tuna Salad Filling

This crunchy tuna salad can be spooned on top of a 225 g (8 oz) jacket potato or used as a sandwich filling with two medium slices of wholemeal bread, for an additional 2½ **POINTS** values per serving.

Serves 2 | Takes 7 minutes | 5½ **POINTS** values per recipe | 161 calories per serving

40 g (1½ oz) reduced fat mayonnaise
60 g (2 oz) low fat natural yogurt
finely grated zest of ½ a lemon
200 g can tuna in spring water, drained

½ red pepper, de-seeded and diced
75 g (2¾ oz) cucumber, diced
freshly ground black pepper

1 Mix the mayonnaise and yogurt with the lemon zest in a small bowl.

2 Stir the tuna into the mayonnaise mixture. Add the red pepper and cucumber and mix through.

3 Season to taste with the black pepper and serve at room temperature rather than chilled to fully enjoy the flavours.

Athol Brose with Nectarines

Athol Brose is a Scottish dessert traditionally made with oats, cream and whisky. Try our equally tasty but lower *POINTS* value version.

Serves 4 | Takes 15 minutes to prepare, 15 minutes to cook + chilling | 10 *POINTS* values per recipe
175 calories per serving | ❤

50 g (1¾ oz) porridge oats
25 g (1 oz) demerara sugar
1 tablespoon clear honey

3 tablespoons whisky
200 g (7 oz) 0% fat Greek yogurt
3 nectarines, sliced

1   Preheat the oven to Gas Mark 4/180°C/fan oven 160°C. Mix together the porridge oats and demerara sugar and spread out on to a non stick baking tray. Bake for 15 minutes and then transfer to a mixing bowl. Stir in the honey and whisky. Allow to cool.

2   When cool, beat in the yogurt, then spoon into four individual stem glasses, alternating with slices of nectarines. Chill for at least 1 hour before serving.

Summer Fruit Frozen Yogurt

This wonderful summer dessert will keep in the freezer for several weeks.

Serves 4 | Takes 5 minutes + thawing + freezing | 3½ *POINTS* values per recipe
62 calories per serving | ❤ | ❄

250 g (9 oz) frozen summer fruits
250 g (9 oz) low fat natural yogurt

3 tablespoons granulated artificial sweetener
1 teaspoon lemon juice

1 Remove the summer fruits from the freezer about an hour before you want to start the recipe and leave them to thaw slightly.

2 Put the slightly thawed summer fruits and their juices in a food processor with the yogurt, sweetener and lemon juice. Blend until well combined. (You can also do this by hand or with a hand held electric beater.)

3 Transfer the mixture to a shallow, freezer proof, lidded plastic container. Cover and freeze for around 6 hours. During that time, beat it with a hand held whisk after 1 hour then every 45 minutes or so until frozen (about 4 hours). Alternatively, freeze in an ice cream maker following the manufacturer's instructions.

4 Ideally, serve the frozen yogurt about 6 hours after making it. If not serving the same day, remove from the freezer 30–45 minutes before serving to soften slightly.

Tip

To remember to beat the yogurt regularly while it's freezing, set the timer on your oven for each 40 minutes.

September
October
November

Autumn

Garlicky Mushroom Soup

NEW RECIPE

Use dark gilled open cup mushrooms to give this soup the best flavour – the large value packs of mushrooms sold in supermarkets are ideal.

Serves 4 | Takes 15 minutes to prepare, 10 minutes to cook | 4½ *POINTS* values per recipe
97 calories per serving | ❷ | ❄ recommended

15 g (½ oz) low fat spread
600 g (1 lb 5 oz) open cup mushrooms, chopped roughly
3 garlic cloves, crushed
850 ml (30 fl oz) hot vegetable stock
25 g (1 oz) plain flour
300 ml (10 fl oz) skimmed milk

freshly ground black pepper

To serve
4 tablespoons very low fat fromage frais
2 tablespoons snipped fresh chives

1   Melt the low fat spread in a large, lidded, non stick saucepan and stir in the mushrooms and garlic and season with black pepper, stirring to coat. Add 4 tablespoons of the stock, cover the pan and cook for 5 minutes until the mushrooms are juicy and soft.

2   Stir in the flour and cook for 1 minute, then gradually add the remaining stock and milk. Bring to the boil, cover and simmer for 10 minutes.

3   Transfer the soup to a liquidiser, or use a hand held blender, and blend until smooth.

4   Serve topped with the fromage frais and chives.

One Pot Italian Beef Stew

This is a great all-in-one filling family casserole, containing meat, vegetables and pasta.

Serves 4 | Takes 25 minutes to prepare, 1 hour 50 minutes hours to cook | 22½ *POINTS* values per recipe
315 calories per serving | ❋ (before adding the pasta)

low fat cooking spray
600 g (1 lb 5 oz) lean beef stewing steak, diced
1 large onion, sliced
6 garlic cloves
1 tablespoon fresh chopped rosemary
12 black olives in brine, drained

400 g can chopped tomatoes
1 litre (35 fl oz) beef stock
125 g (4½ oz) dried wholemeal pasta shapes, e.g. fusilli
freshly ground black pepper

1 Preheat the oven to Gas Mark 1/140°C/ fan oven 120°C.

2 Heat a non stick frying pan, spray with the cooking spray and brown the beef in two batches, transferring the meat to a plate as it is done.

3 Heat a large, lidded, flameproof and ovenproof casserole dish, spray with the cooking spray and brown the onion, adding a splash of water if it starts to stick.

4 Add the whole garlic cloves, rosemary, olives and tomatoes to the casserole dish. Pour a little of the stock into the frying pan and stir to release the meat browning juices, then add this to the casserole, along with the rest of the stock. Add the beef to the casserole and bring it to a simmer. Cover and transfer to the oven to cook for 1½ hours.

5 Stir the pasta into the casserole, pushing it down into the liquid. Replace the lid and return the casserole to the oven to cook for 15–20 minutes, until the pasta is tender. Season and serve immediately.

Chicken and Mushroom Pie

Serve this richly flavoured pie with a colourful mixture of zero **POINTS** value carrots, broccoli and cauliflower, adding 100 g (3½ oz) cooked potatoes per person, for an extra 1 **POINTS** value per serving.

Serves 4 | Takes 25 minutes to prepare + 30 minutes chilling, 25 minutes to cook | 19½ **POINTS** values per recipe
353 calories per serving | ❋

For the pastry
150 g (5½ oz) plain flour
a pinch of salt
65 g (2¼ oz) low fat spread

For the filling
low fat cooking spray
2 x 165 g (5¾ oz) skinless boneless chicken breasts, diced
1 onion, sliced thinly

2 garlic cloves, crushed
250 g (9 oz) closed cup mushrooms, quartered
1 heaped tablespoon plain flour
1 tablespoon chopped fresh sage or 1 teaspoon dried sage
10 g (¼ oz) porcini mushrooms, snipped into small pieces
100 ml (3½ fl oz) white wine
300 ml (10 fl oz) chicken stock
1 tablespoon skimmed milk, to brush
salt and freshly ground black pepper

1 Sift the flour and salt into a bowl. Rub in the low fat spread until the mixture resembles breadcrumbs. Add just enough cold water to bring the dough together. Shape into a disc, wrap in clingfilm and chill for 30 minutes.

2 Preheat the oven to Gas Mark 5/190°C/fan oven 170°C.

3 Heat a large, lidded, non stick frying pan, spray with the cooking spray and brown the chicken pieces. You may need to do this in batches. Remove the chicken to a plate.

4 In the same frying pan, soften the onion for 3 minutes before adding the garlic and mushrooms. Cook for a further 2 minutes. Stir in the flour, sage and porcini mushrooms, then gradually blend in the wine and chicken stock. Return the chicken to the pan. Bring to the boil, season, then cover and simmer for 15 minutes. Tip into a ceramic pie dish with a lip and cool for 10 minutes.

5 Roll out the pastry to a circle slightly larger than the top of the dish. Cut a narrow strip of pastry from around the outside, brush the edge of the dish with water and press the pastry strip onto the lip of the dish. Dampen the pastry border, then lift the pastry lid into place. Press down well and trim the edges. Use a fork to stamp a pattern around the edge, and use the pastry trimmings to decorate the top. Brush with the milk and then bake the pie for 25 minutes until crisp and golden.

Baked Marrow Gratin

This is easier to make than it looks and a great way to use marrows or even overgrown courgettes.

Serves 4 | Takes 40 minutes to prepare, 30 minutes to cook | 13 **POINTS** values per recipe
230 calories per serving | ❋ (before adding cheese)

1 kg (2 lb 4 oz) marrow, halved lengthways and de-seeded
low fat cooking spray
2 onions, chopped finely
2 garlic cloves, crushed
200 g (7 oz) lean lamb mince
1 teaspoon mixed dried herbs
2 teaspoons Worcestershire sauce

a dash of Tabasco sauce
400 g can chopped tomatoes
50 g (1¾ oz) dried apricots or prunes, chopped finely
a small bunch of fresh parsley or mint, chopped
50 g (1¾ oz) reduced fat mature Cheddar cheese, grated
salt and freshly ground black pepper

1 Preheat the oven to Gas Mark 6/200°C/fan oven 180°C.
   Scoop out some of the marrow flesh but leave at least
   5 mm (¼ inch) inside the skin to make a firm shell. Chop
   the flesh finely.

2 Heat a large, lidded, non stick frying pan, spray with the
   cooking spray and gently fry the onions and garlic for
   4 minutes, until softened. Add a little water if necessary
   to prevent them from sticking.

3 Add the mince and break it up with a wooden spoon.
   Season and cook for another 3–4 minutes, until browned
   all over, then add the chopped marrow and stir together
   for another minute.

4 Add all the other ingredients except the cheese and
   bring to a simmer. Cover and cook for 10 minutes.

5 Place the marrow cases side by side in an oven dish or
   deep tray. Pile the mixture into the marrow cases. Add
   about 150 ml (¼ pint) of cold water to the oven dish, then
   cover with foil. Bake for 20 minutes.

6 Remove the foil, scatter over the cheese and bake for
   10 minutes, until the cheese is melted. Divide each
   marrow case into two and serve.

Chinese Stir Fried Pork

This tasty pork mince can be served with 60 g (2 oz) of dried egg noodles or brown rice per person, cooked according to packet instructions, for an extra 3 *POINTS* values per serving. Alternatively, serve with a pile of large crisp lettuce leaves (from an Iceberg lettuce or similar) to wrap around the pork mixture for no additional *POINTS* values.

Serves 4 | Takes 20 minutes to prepare | 19 *POINTS* values per recipe
265 calories per serving | ❄ (before adding the beansprouts)

low fat cooking spray
500 g (1 lb 2 oz) lean pork mince
1 red pepper, de-seeded and sliced
1 yellow pepper, de-seeded and sliced
2 tablespoons Chinese 5-spice powder

250 g (9 oz) mushrooms, sliced
150 ml (5 fl oz) oyster sauce
200 ml (7 fl oz) boiling water
200 g (7 oz) beansprouts, rinsed

1 Heat a wok or large non stick frying pan until hot and spray with the cooking spray. Add the pork mince and stir fry for 5 minutes, stirring to break up the mince.

2 Add the peppers and Chinese 5-spice and cook for a further 2 minutes, stirring. Mix in the mushrooms and cook for 2 more minutes then add the oyster sauce and water and simmer for 2 minutes.

3 Stir in the beansprouts and cook for just long enough to heat them through, without losing their crunch. Serve immediately.

♥ Variation

Replace the pork mince with the same amount of Quorn mince, adding with the peppers in step 2, and use black bean sauce in place of the oyster sauce, for 2½ *POINTS* values per serving.

Cheese and Corn Soufflé

You can also make this with fresh sweetcorn. Bring a pan of water to the boil and cook 2 sweetcorn cobs until tender. Drain, cut away the sweetcorn and use as in step 3.

Serves 2 | Takes 10 minutes to prepare, 1 hour to cook | 10½ *POINTS* values per recipe
321 calories per serving | ⊙

low fat cooking spray
2 eggs
25 g (1 oz) plain flour
200 ml (7 fl oz) skimmed milk

200 g (7 oz) canned sweetcorn, drained
60 g (2 oz) reduced fat Cheddar cheese, grated
½ green pepper, de-seeded and chopped
salt and freshly ground black pepper

1 Preheat the oven to Gas Mark 4/180°C/fan oven 160°C. Spray a 700 ml (1¼ pint) soufflé dish (or 2 x 350 ml/12 fl oz) dishes) with the cooking spray.

2 Whisk the eggs with the flour, then gradually whisk in the milk.

3 Stir in the sweetcorn, cheese and green pepper and season.

4 Pour into the dish or dishes and bake for 1 hour or until puffed up and golden. (Individual soufflés will take around 45 minutes.)

Saffron Seafood Risotto

Seafood should be in season right now, but if you cannot find fresh ingredients use frozen instead.

Serves 4 | Takes 10 minutes to prepare, 35 minutes to cook | 17½ **POINTS** values per recipe

356 calories per serving

low fat cooking spray
3 garlic cloves, crushed
3 leeks, washed and sliced finely
1 red pepper, de-seeded and diced
½ teaspoon fennel seeds, crushed or ground
250 g (9 oz) dried brown rice
a good pinch of saffron strands

1.2 litres (2 pints) fish, chicken or vegetable stock
400 g (14 oz) frozen or fresh mixed seafood, defrosted if necessary
a bunch of fresh parsley, chopped
a few sprigs of fresh dill, chopped
freshly ground black pepper
lemon wedges, to serve

1 Heat a large, lidded, non stick pan, spray with the cooking spray and stir fry the garlic, leeks and pepper with 100 ml (3½ fl oz) of water for 5 minutes, or until softened.

2 Add the fennel seeds, brown rice and saffron and stir, then add the stock and stir again. Cover the pan and leave on a low heat for 30 minutes, or until nearly all the stock has been absorbed.

3 Add the seafood and fresh herbs and stir through. Replace the lid and cook for a further 5 minutes, or until the seafood is heated through. Season with black pepper and serve with lemon wedges.

Tip

If you don't have saffron strands, use a teaspoon of ground turmeric instead.

♥ Variation

For a vegetarian version, replace the seafood mixture with 200 g (7 oz) frozen peas, for 4 **POINTS** values per serving.

Plum Charlotte

This traditional pudding is such a treat.

Serves 4 | Takes 25 minutes to prepare, 35 minutes to cook | 12½ **POINTS** values per recipe
198 calories per serving | ♥

500 g (1 lb 2 oz) plums, halved and pitted
zest and juice of an orange
1 teaspoon cinnamon

4 tablespoons artificial sweetener
25 g (1 oz) low fat spread, melted
7 medium slices white bread, crusts removed

1   Preheat the oven to Gas Mark 4/180°C/fan oven 160°C.

2   Put the plums into a saucepan with the orange zest and juice and cinnamon. Add 5 tablespoons of water, then simmer until the plums are tender – about 10 minutes. Sweeten to taste with the artificial sweetener. (Some plums are sweeter than others, so will need less sweetener).

3   Brush a 15 cm (6 inch) straight sided baking dish or cake tin with the low fat spread. Brush the rest of the low fat spread lightly over the slices of bread. Place one slice in the base of the dish or tin, reserve one for the top, then fit the rest of the slices around the sides, easing them into place and cutting them to fit so that there are no spaces. Spoon in the plums and place the remaining slice of bread on top, folding the bread around the sides over to enclose the plum filling.

4   Bake for 30–35 minutes. Cool for a few minutes, then serve.

Baked Pears with Honey, Nutmeg and Lemon

NEW RECIPE (2 POINTS VALUE)

A super speedy pudding that smells simply divine when the foil parcels are opened.

Serves 2 | Takes 5 minutes to prepare, 10 minutes to cook | 4½ *POINTS* values per recipe
127 calories per serving | ✔

2 slightly under ripe pears, cored
finely grated zest and juice of ½ a small lemon
15 g (½ oz) currants

2 rounded teaspoons clear honey
freshly grated nutmeg
100 g (3½ oz) 0% fat Greek yogurt

1   Preheat the oven to Gas Mark 6/200°C/fan oven 180°C. Cut two large squares of foil from a roll.

2   Cut each pear into eight wedges and divide equally between the two foil squares. Divide the lemon zest and juice and currants between the parcels, then drizzle each one with a rounded teaspoon of honey. Add a few gratings of nutmeg then crimp the edges of the foil together to seal the parcels.

3   Place on a baking tray and bake for 10 minutes.

4   To serve, open up the foil parcels, being careful not to burn yourself on any steam, and serve with the yogurt.

Autumn

September
October
November

Harvest Gold Soup

A warming, filling soup for those colder autumn days.

Serves 4 | Takes 20 minutes to prepare, 30 minutes to cook | 12 **POINTS** values per recipe
319 calories per serving | ❶ | ❋

low fat cooking spray
2 onions, chopped
2 garlic cloves, crushed
600 g (1 lb 5 oz) sweet potatoes, scrubbed and chopped roughly
1 butternut squash or 1 small to medium pumpkin, peeled, de-seeded and chopped roughly

100 g (3½ oz) red lentils
a pinch of dried chilli flakes, optional
1.2 litres (2 pints) vegetable stock
salt and freshly ground black pepper
red or green chillies, chopped finely, to serve, optional

1   Heat a large, lidded saucepan, spray with the cooking spray, then gently stir fry the onions and garlic with 4 tablespoons of water until softened.

2   Add the sweet potatoes and squash or pumpkin, lentils, chilli flakes, if using, and stock. Cover and bring to the boil. Turn down the heat and simmer for 20 minutes, or until the vegetables are tender.

3   Liquidise in a blender or use a hand held blender. Season to taste and serve sprinkled with chopped chilli to garnish, if using.

Tip

A handful of lentils is a good addition to most vegetarian soups. They add valuable protein and help to thicken the soup, which makes it extra satisfying.

❶ Variation

You can use the same volume of potatoes instead of sweet potatoes and carrots instead of squash or pumpkin. The **POINTS** values per serving will remain the same.

Creamy Smoked Mackerel Pasta

This is a simple fast dish that tastes absolutely delicious. Serve with a selection of seasonal steamed zero *POINTS* value vegetables, if you wish.

Serves 4 | Takes 5 minutes to prepare, 10 minutes to cook | 35 *POINTS* values per recipe | 530 calories per serving

240 g (8½ oz) dried pasta
325 g (11½ oz) smoked mackerel, flaked
4 tablespoons half fat crème fraîche

1 pack of fresh parsley, chopped
salt and freshly ground black pepper

1   Bring a pan of water to the boil and cook the pasta according to the packet instructions or until tender. Drain.

2   Toss the pasta with the other ingredients and serve immediately in warmed bowls.

Butternut Squash and Goat's Cheese Strudel

Just the thing for a smart vegetarian main course.

Serves 4 | Takes 40 minutes to prepare, 15 minutes to cook | 18½ _POINTS_ values per recipe
284 calories per serving | ❤ | ✳ (before cooking)

600 g (1lb 5 oz) butternut squash, peeled, de-seeded and diced
1 red pepper, de-seeded and cut into 1 cm (½ inch) dice
low fat cooking spray
1 large leek, trimmed, washed and sliced
25 g (1 oz) pecans, chopped roughly
2 x 45 g sheets filo pastry

100 g (3½ oz) soft rinded goat's cheese, diced
salt and freshly ground black pepper

To serve
150 g carton 0% fat Greek yogurt
1 small garlic clove, crushed
1 tablespoon snipped chives

1   Preheat the oven to Gas Mark 7/220°C/fan oven 200°C. Mix the squash and red pepper together, season and spread on a large baking tray. Lightly mist with the cooking spray and roast for 10 minutes.

2   Stir the leek into the vegetables and roast for a further 5 minutes, then add the pecans and cook for a further 5 minutes. Remove and cool slightly.

3   Cut the sheets of filo pastry in sixths to create 12 smaller rectangles. For each strudel, layer up three of these pieces, lightly spraying with the cooking spray between each layer. Spoon a quarter of the vegetables onto each pastry rectangle and divide the goat's cheese between them.

4   Roll each pastry up into a log, tucking in the ends to hold in the filling. Transfer to a baking sheet, lightly mist with the cooking spray and bake for 15 minutes until crisp.

5   Mix the yogurt with the garlic, chives and seasoning and serve with the strudels.

Kofta in Red Curry Sauce

A stunning beef curry that is just right for an autumn evening in.

Serves 2 | Takes 20 minutes to prepare + chilling, 20 minutes to cook | 10 *POINTS* values per recipe
305 calories per serving | ✔ (meatballs and sauce separately if uncooked)

200 g (7 oz) lean beef mince
1 small onion, chopped finely
1 garlic clove, chopped
1 tablespoon chopped fresh root ginger
½ teaspoon ground cumin
1 tablespoon chopped fresh coriander, plus extra
  to garnish
1 small egg, beaten lightly
salt and freshly ground black pepper

For the red curry sauce
low fat cooking spray
1 onion, chopped finely
2 garlic cloves, chopped finely
1 tablespoon tandoori curry powder
1 teaspoon ground coriander
1 teaspoon ground cumin
400 g can chopped tomatoes
4 tablespoons 0% fat Greek yogurt

1   Put the beef, onion, garlic, ginger, cumin, coriander and egg in a food processor. Season and blend to a coarse paste. Using wet hands, shape the mixture into walnut size balls. Put them on a plate and chill, covered, for about 30 minutes.

2   To make the sauce, heat a lidded, non stick frying pan, spray with the cooking spray and fry the onion for 7 minutes, adding a little water if it starts to stick. Add the garlic and spices and cook for 30 seconds.

3   Pour in the tomatoes and add 5 tablespoons of water. Bring to the boil then reduce the heat to simmering point. Arrange the meatballs in the pan, cover, and simmer for 15–20 minutes, turning occasionally and adding a little water if the sauce looks too dry, until the meatballs are cooked through.

4   When the meatballs are cooked, remove them from the pan using a slotted spoon and arrange on two plates. Stir the yogurt into the pan and season. Heat through gently then spoon the sauce over the meatballs. Garnish with the extra coriander.

Garlic Chicken Casserole

A soothing chicken dish, infused with the flavour of garlic. Serve with mashed butternut squash (see Tip), for no additional *POINTS* values.

Serves 6 | Takes 10 minutes to prepare, 1 hour to cook | 15½ *POINTS* values per recipe | 180 calories per serving

low fat cooking spray
6 x 150 g (5½ oz) skinless boneless chicken breasts
3 whole heads of garlic
a small bunch of thyme, woody stems removed and leaves chopped

a few rosemary sprigs, woody stems removed and leaves chopped
100 ml (3½ fl oz) dry white wine
400 ml (14 fl oz) chicken stock
salt and freshly ground black pepper
a small bunch of fresh parsley, chopped, to garnish

1   Preheat the oven to Gas Mark 4/180°C/fan oven 160°C. Heat a large, flameproof and ovenproof casserole, spray with the cooking spray, then fry the chicken breasts gently for 5–6 minutes until browned all over. You may need to do this in batches.

2   Return all the chicken to the casserole. Separate the cloves of garlic, then peel and scatter them over the top of the chicken with the herbs and seasoning. Pour over the wine and stock, cover the casserole and bake in the oven for 1 hour.

3   Serve hot, sprinkled with the parsley.

Tip

To make a butternut squash mash, cut a butternut squash in half and scoop out the seeds. Cut each half into wedges and spray with low fat cooking spray. Season and place skin side down on a roasting tray. Roast at Gas Mark 7/220° C/fan oven 200°C for 20–25 minutes. When cool enough to handle, scoop out the flesh, mash, then season.

Stir Fried Chinese Vegetables

Serving a side dish of these Oriental style vegetables is a great way of livening up a piece of plainly cooked fish or meat without adding any **POINTS** values.

Serves 2 | Takes 15 minutes | 0 **POINTS** values per recipe | 69 calories per serving | ✔

low fat cooking spray
100 g (3½ oz) mushrooms, quartered
75 g (2¾ oz) mange tout
1 garlic clove, sliced

2.5 cm (1 inch) fresh root ginger, peeled and cut into slivers
½ head Chinese leaf, shredded coarsely
1 tablespoon soy sauce

1 Heat a lidded wok or large, lidded, non stick frying pan until hot and spray with the cooking spray. Add the mushrooms and mange tout plus 1 tablespoon of water and stir fry for 4 minutes.

2 Add the garlic and ginger and cook for 1 minute.

3 Add the Chinese leaf, soy sauce and 1 tablespoon of water to the pan.

4 Cover and cook for 3 minutes until the vegetables are tender. Serve immediately.

Variation

Turn this into a low **POINTS** value vegetable chow mein by adding 100 g (3½ oz) baby corn in step 1, plus 75 g (2¾ oz) drained water chestnuts in step 2. Toss the cooked vegetables through 300 g (10½ oz) cooked egg noodles (125 g/4½ oz dried weight), for 3 **POINTS** values per serving.

Hallowe'en Hubble Bubble Casserole

This sausage casserole is a popular choice for feeding a crowd of friends in cold weather. Serve with a 225 g (8 oz) baked potato per person, for an extra 2½ **POINTS** values per serving.

Serves 8 | Takes 15 minutes to prepare, 20 minutes to cook | 30 **POINTS** values per recipe
249 calories per serving | ❄

16 thick low fat sausages
low fat cooking spray
6 rashers lean back bacon, chopped
2 x 415 g cans reduced sugar and salt baked beans

400 g can chopped tomatoes
1 tablespoon Worcestershire sauce
25 g (1 oz) dark brown soft sugar
salt and freshly ground black pepper

1   Twist each sausage into two smaller pieces and cut apart. Heat a non stick frying pan, spray with the cooking spray, add half the sausages and brown for 3–4 minutes, shaking the pan occasionally so that they colour evenly.

2   Tip the cooked sausages into a flameproof casserole dish, then brown the remaining sausages in the same way and add these to the casserole.

3   Fry the bacon for 2 minutes in the frying pan, then stir it into the sausages, adding the baked beans, chopped tomatoes, Worcestershire sauce, sugar and seasoning. Bring to a simmer, cover and cook gently for 20 minutes.

Cinnamon Apple Flan

A fabulous fruit tart that is delicious served with a 60 g (2 oz) scoop of low fat vanilla ice cream per person, for an extra 1 *POINTS* value per serving.

Serves 6 | Takes 20 minutes to prepare, 20 minutes to cook + cooling | 15½ *POINTS* values per recipe
173 calories per scone | ❤

110 g (4 oz) plain flour
50 g (1¾ oz) low fat spread
75 g (2¾ oz) caster sugar

3 cooking apples, peeled, cored and sliced thinly
1 teaspoon ground cinnamon
low fat cooking spray

1 Preheat the oven to Gas Mark 5/190°C/fan oven 170°C and place a baking tray in the oven to preheat.

2 Sift the flour into a mixing bowl and rub in the low fat spread until the mixture resembles breadcrumbs. Stir in 50 g (1¾ oz) of the sugar. Press firmly into a loose based 23 cm (9 inch) flan tin. Arrange the apple slices on top, in a circular pattern if you want the flan to look decorative, or just randomly if you prefer a rustic look.

3 Mix the rest of the caster sugar with the cinnamon and sprinkle evenly over the apples. Spray with the cooking spray and bake the flan on the hot tray for 30 minutes, until the juices are bubbling and the edges of the apple are slightly caramelised.

4 Leave to cool before removing from the tin. Cut into wedges and serve.

Chocolate Hallowe'en Cupcakes

We topped these cupcakes with a spooky web design and plastic spiders for some sweet Hallowe'en fun.

Serves 24 | Takes 20 minutes to prepare, 20 minute to cook | 36 **POINTS** values per recipe
98 calories per serving | ❷

250 g (9 oz) plain flour
100 g (3½ oz) cocoa powder
25 g (1 oz) cornflour
1 teaspoon baking powder
10 tablespoons artificial sweetener
2 egg whites
3 level tablespoons runny honey

For the frosting
150 g (5½ oz) caster sugar
1 egg white
1 level tablespoon golden syrup

For the icing
50 g (1¾ oz) icing sugar
1–2 teaspoons hot water
1–2 drops orange food colouring

1   Preheat the oven to Gas Mark 4/180°C/fan oven 160°C. Line two 12-hole muffin tins with paper cakes or greaseproof paper.

2   Sift the flour, cocoa powder, cornflour and baking powder into a large bowl and stir in the artificial sweetener.

3   Add the egg whites, 250 ml (9 fl oz) of water and the honey and mix quickly until just combined. Spoon into the muffin papers until each hole is completely full.

4   Bake for 15–20 minutes, or until a skewer inserted in the middle of one of the cakes comes out clean. Allow to cool completely on a wire rack.

5   To make the frosting, heat a medium saucepan of water to boiling. Meanwhile, in a medium metal or glass bowl, using an electric whisk, beat the sugar, 1 tablespoon of cold water and the egg white with the golden syrup. Beat for 1 minute until thickening.

6   Place the bowl of frosting over the saucepan of boiling water and, using an electric whisk, beat at high speed for 4–5 minutes until the mixture forms soft peaks. Remove from the heat and beat until the mixture is thick enough to spread. Frost the muffins.

7   For the icing, sift the sugar and mix to a stiff paste with the water and food colouring. Decorate the muffins to create spiders' webs.

Autumn

September
October
November

Sweet Potato, Leek and Tomato Soup

Sweet potatoes give this vibrantly coloured soup a fabulously velvety texture.

Serves 4 | Takes 15 minutes to prepare, 15 minutes to cook | 6 *POINTS* values per recipe
139 calories per serving | Ⓥ | ❋

low fat cooking spray
2 leeks, trimmed, washed and chopped roughly
400 g (14 oz) sweet potatoes, peeled and diced
400 g can chopped tomatoes
850 ml (30 fl oz) vegetable stock

salt and freshly ground black pepper

To serve
4 tablespoons very low fat plain fromage frais
2 tablespoons snipped fresh chives

1 Heat a large, lidded, non stick saucepan, spray with the cooking spray, add the leeks and stir to coat. Season, and add 2 tablespoons water. Cover the pan and sweat over a medium heat for 5 minutes until softened.

2 Stir in the sweet potatoes, tomatoes and stock, bring to the boil and simmer, covered, for 15 minutes or until the sweet potato is soft.

3 Cool slightly, transfer to a liquidiser, or use a hand held blender, and blend until smooth. Return to the pan to warm through and adjust the seasoning if necessary. Serve topped with a swirl of fromage frais and a scattering of chives.

Creamy Ham and Mushroom Pasta

NEW RECIPE

Serve with a zero *POINTS* value seasonal salad.

Serves 1 | Takes 15 minutes | 5 *POINTS* values per recipe | 327 calories per serving

60 g (2 oz) dried pasta shells
50 g (1¾ oz) frozen peas
low fat cooking spray
100 g (3½ oz) button mushrooms, sliced

30 g (1¼ oz) low fat soft cheese with garlic and herbs
30 g (1¼ oz) wafer thin smoked ham, chopped finely
freshly ground black pepper

1   Bring a pan of water to the boil and cook the pasta for 10–12 minutes until tender, or according to the packet instructions, adding the peas for the last 2 minutes of the cooking time.

2   Meanwhile, heat a non stick pan and spray with the cooking spray. Fry the mushrooms for 3–4 minutes until golden and tender. Mix in the soft cheese, plus 1 tablespoon of the pasta cooking water to give a creamy sauce.

3   Drain the pasta and peas and toss with the mushroom sauce, mixing in the ham. Season to taste with black pepper and serve immediately.

 Variation

Why not try substituting 30 g (1¼ oz) Quorn Deli Ham Style Slices for the wafer thin ham, for the same *POINTS* values per serving.

Bangers and Mash with Onion Gravy

A great traditional, heartening meal that all the family love.

Serves 4 | Takes 15 minutes to prepare, 30 minutes to cook | 16½ **POINTS** values per recipe | 365 calories per serving

low fat cooking spray
4 onions, sliced thinly
1 kg (2 lb 4 oz) potatoes, peeled and chopped roughly
8 thin low fat sausages

100 ml (3½ fl oz) skimmed milk
600 ml (20 fl oz) vegetable stock
1 tablespoon Worcestershire sauce
salt and freshly ground black pepper

1   Spray a large, lidded saucepan with the cooking spray and then add the onions and stir. Season and cover with a piece of baking parchment and then cover the pan so the onions are sealed. Cook over a very low heat for 30 minutes, or until the onions are soft and starting to brown. Preheat the oven to Gas Mark 6/200°C/fan oven 180°C.

2   Meanwhile, bring a pan of water to the boil, add the potatoes and boil for 20–30 minutes, until tender when you insert the point of a knife.

3   Put the sausages on a non stick baking tray and cook in the oven for 25 minutes, turning occasionally.

4   Drain the potatoes and mash them with the milk and seasoning. Keep warm.

5   Finish the onion gravy by removing the lid and the paper from the onions and adding the stock and Worcestershire sauce. Bring to the boil and simmer on a high heat for a few minutes or until thickened, then serve with the bangers and mash, allowing two sausages per person.

Huntsman Chicken

A real cold weather dish with a delicious warming tangy sauce. Serve with seasonal steamed zero *POINTS* value vegetables.

Serves 4 | Takes 20 minutes to prepare, 30 minutes to cook | 17 *POINTS* values per recipe
240 calories per serving | ❄

4 x 150 g (5½ oz) skinless boneless chicken breasts
4 rashers lean back bacon
1 tablespoon finely chopped fresh flat leaf parsley,
 to serve

For the sauce
low fat cooking spray
20 silverskin onions, drained and rinsed

1 garlic clove, crushed
1 tablespoon light brown sugar
2 tablespoons cider vinegar
1 tablespoon tomato ketchup
2 teaspoons Dijon mustard
1 teaspoon mild chilli powder
1 tablespoon tomato purée
1 tablespoon brown sauce

1 Preheat the oven to Gas Mark 5/190°C/fan oven 170°C.

2 To make the sauce, heat a non stick saucepan and spray with the cooking spray. Cook the onions and garlic for 3–4 minutes until lightly browned. Add the remaining ingredients and 125 ml (4 fl oz) of water and bring to the boil. Simmer for 5 minutes until beginning to thicken. Set aside.

3 Wrap each chicken breast with a rasher of bacon and put into an ovenproof dish. Pour over the sauce and bake in the oven for 30 minutes until cooked. Sprinkle with parsley and serve.

❤ Variation

For a vegetarian version, use 4 Quorn chicken style fillets and 4 Quorn style bacon rashers, wrapping each fillet in one rasher and cooking with the sauce, for a *POINTS* value of 1½ per serving.

Baked Haddock with Tomatoes

A quick, no hassle recipe. Except for the fish, you will probably have all the ingredients in your storecupboard.

Serves 4 | Takes 40 minutes to prepare, 40 minutes to cook | 13½ **POINTS** values per recipe | 265 calories per serving

800 g (1 lb 11 oz) potatoes, peeled and chopped roughly
low fat cooking spray
2 onions, sliced thinly
2 garlic cloves, sliced thinly
4 haddock fillets, weighing approximately 400 g (14 oz) in total

400 g can chopped tomatoes
1 tablespoon balsamic vinegar or lemon juice
salt and freshly ground black pepper
chopped parsley, to garnish (optional)

1   Bring a pan of water to the boil and cook the potatoes until tender, approximately 25 minutes. Drain.

2   Preheat the oven to Gas Mark 3/170°C/fan oven 150°C.

3   Heat a non stick frying pan and spray with the cooking spray, then fry the onions and garlic for 4 minutes until softened, adding a splash of water if they start to stick.

4   Spray an ovenproof dish with the cooking spray and add the haddock fillets, placing them skin side down. Scatter the onions and garlic over the top, pour over the tomatoes, vinegar or lemon juice and 125 ml (4 fl oz) of water and season well. Bake for 35–40 minutes.

5   To serve, mash the potatoes, season and then spoon on to four plates and top with a piece of haddock and some of the sauce. Garnish with chopped parsley, if using.

Variation

You could serve the haddock with 225 g (8 oz) cooked pasta or 100 g (3½ oz) couscous per person instead of the potatoes. The **POINTS** values per serving will be 2 with pasta, 2½ with couscous.

Autumn Vegetable Gratin

Use your choice of seasonal root vegetables for this lovely gratin.

Serves 4 | Takes 10 minutes to prepare, 30 minutes to cook | 5½ *POINTS* values per recipe
95 calories per serving | ◯

250 g (9 oz) pumpkin, rind and seeds removed, flesh diced
350 g (12 oz) root vegetables, such as carrots or swedes (not parsnips), peeled and chopped into chunks
1 garlic clove, crushed
125 ml (4 fl oz) medium sherry

1 tablespoon cornflour
1 teaspoon dried mixed herbs
1 tablespoon freshly grated Parmesan cheese
25 g (1 oz) fresh breadcrumbs
salt and freshly ground black pepper

1 Place the pumpkin, root vegetables and garlic in a large pan and cover with water. Bring to the boil and simmer until all the vegetables are tender. This will take about 20 minutes, depending on your choice of root vegetables. Preheat the grill to high.

2 Drain the vegetables, reserving the cooking water, and place in a gratin dish.

3 Add enough of the vegetable water to the sherry to make 400 ml (14 fl oz). Pour into a saucepan and heat.

4 Mix the cornflour with a little cold water and add it to the sherry water. Cook until slightly thickened.

5 Add the herbs and season well. Pour over the vegetables.

6 Sprinkle the Parmesan and breadcrumbs over the top of the gratin and grill for about 10 minutes, until brown on top.

Variation

You can replace the pumpkin with any other type of squash. The *POINTS* values will remain the same.

Rich Beef and Prune Casserole

Serve this rich autumnal casserole with 100 g (3½ oz) of boiled floury potatoes per person to soak up all the delicious juices, for an additional 1 *POINTS* value per serving.

Serves 6 | Takes 15 minutes to prepare, 1¼ hours to cook | 12 *POINTS* values per recipe
167 calories per serving | ❀

low fat cooking spray
500 g (1 lb 2 oz) rump steak, cut into 2 cm (¾ inch) cubes
6 small onions or shallots, quartered
6 carrots, peeled and sliced thickly
100 g (3½ oz) prunes in natural juice (check that there are no stones)

400 g can chopped tomatoes
600 ml (20 fl oz) beef or vegetable stock
grated zest of an orange
a few sprigs of fresh thyme or 1 teaspoon dried thyme
1 bay leaf
salt and freshly ground black pepper

1 Heat a large, lidded, flameproof casserole dish, spray with the cooking spray and add the meat in three batches. Stir fry each batch until browned all over, then season and remove to a plate while you brown the other batches.

2 Return all the meat to the casserole dish and add all the other ingredients. Stir, scraping any bits from the bottom of the pan.

3 Bring to the boil, then turn down to a low simmer, cover, and leave to cook for 1 hour.

V Variation

A lovely vegetarian version can be made by substituting 450 g (1 lb) mushrooms for the meat and substituting vegetable stock for the beef stock. Cook for 1 hour, for ½ *POINTS* value per serving.

Fruity Cinnamon Rice Pudding

A quick hob-cooked version of rice pudding, flavoured with sweet cinnamon.

Serves 2 | Takes 20 minutes | 7½ **POINTS** values per recipe | 254 calories per serving | ⓥ

75 g (2¾ oz) arborio (risotto) rice
300 ml (10 fl oz) skimmed milk
¾ teaspoon ground cinnamon

60 g (2 oz) dried apricots, diced
1 tablespoon caster sugar

1 Place the rice in a non stick saucepan with the milk, cinnamon and 100 ml (3½ fl oz) of water. Bring to the boil, stirring occasionally so that the rice doesn't stick to the base of the pan, especially towards the end of the cooking time.

2 Simmer for about 18 minutes until most of the liquid has been absorbed and the rice is tender. It should have a soft, slightly soupy consistency when ready.

3 Just before serving stir in the apricots and sugar.

Baked Nutmeg Custard Pots

These velvety smooth custard pots can be served topped with 60 g (2 oz) drained canned apricots in natural juice per person, for an extra ½ **POINTS** value per serving.

Serves 6 | Takes 15 minutes to prepare, 20 minutes to cook | 8½ **POINTS** values per recipe
100 calories per serving | ◉

425 ml (15 fl oz) skimmed milk
60 g (2 oz) low fat soft cheese
3 eggs, plus 1 egg yolk, beaten

1 teaspoon vanilla extract
5 tablespoons granulated artificial sweetener
¼ whole nutmeg

1 Preheat the oven to Gas Mark 3/160°C/ fan oven 140°C. Gradually bring the milk up to simmering point in a saucepan, and put the kettle on to boil.

2 Meanwhile, place the soft cheese in a mixing bowl and slowly mix in the beaten eggs until smooth using a wooden spoon. Make sure that the mixture doesn't become frothy, causing air bubbles in the custard pots.

3 Slowly pour the hot milk over the egg mixture, mixing until smooth. Stir in the vanilla and sweetener.

4 Place six ramekin dishes in a roasting tin and divide the egg mixture between them, pouring it through a sieve to remove any eggy threads that would spoil the texture.

5 Grate plenty of fresh nutmeg on to the custards and then place the roasting tin in the oven. Pour boiling water into the tin around the ramekins and bake for about 20 minutes, until the custards feel just firm to the touch, but are still slightly wobbly in the centre.

6 Carefully lift the ramekins out of the hot water bath using a fish slice. Let them cool slightly before eating them warm, or cool completely and then chill until ready to serve.

Index

A
apple flan, cinnamon 157
apricot scones, easy 117
asparagus and leek tart 78
athol brose with nectarines 130
aubergine parmigiana 122
autumn vegetable gratin 169

B
Baileys mousse 17
baked haddock with tomatoes 168
baked marrow gratin 138
baked nutmeg custard pots 173
baked pears with honey, nutmeg and
     lemon 145
banana and chocolate muffins 60
bangers and mash with onion gravy 164
beans:
     Hallowe'en hubble bubble
          casserole 156
     quick chorizo and bean chilli 120
     warm broad bean and smoked ham
          pittas 92
beef:
     beef and Guinness casserole 58
     beef hotpot 16
     beef rogan josh 38
     kofta in red curry sauce 152
     Mexican tortillas with spicy beef 126
     one pot Italian beef stew 135
     pastrami and ricotta pasta 116
     peppered steak with balsamic
          onions 24
     rich beef and prune casserole 170
     roast beef with Yorkshires 41
     sesame beef salad 94
     spicy Swedish meatballs 80
blueberry hotcakes 106
braised chicken with red cabbage 10
braised pork casserole 15
broad bean and smoked ham pittas,
     warm 92
burgers:
     minty lamb burgers 113
     spicy pork and pineapple burgers 70
butterflied tandoori chicken 100
butternut squash and goat's cheese
     strudel 151

C
cabbage, braised chicken with red 10

Cajun fish cakes 68
cakes:
     carrot cake traybake 102
     chocolate Hallowe'en cupcakes 158
cannelloni 40
carrot cake traybake 102
casseroles:
     beef and Guinness casserole 58
     beef hotpot 16
     braised pork casserole 15
     garlic chicken casserole 154
     Hallowe'en hubble bubble
          casserole 156
     rich beef and prune casserole 170
     winter pork ragù 30
     winter vegetable casserole with spicy
          dumplings 14
cauliflower:
     cauliflower cheese 37
     spiced cauliflower pasta 25
celeriac soup, creamy 22
cheat's chicken makhani 54
cheese:
     aubergine parmigiana 122
     butternut squash and goat's cheese
          strudel 151
     cauliflower cheese 37
     cheese and corn soufflé 141
     pastrami and ricotta pasta 116
chestnut soup with sage and caraway
     croûtons 8
chicken:
     braised chicken with red cabbage 10
     butterflied tandoori chicken 100
     cheat's chicken makhani 54
     chicken and mushroom pie 136
     chicken and spring vegetable
          fricassee 71
     chicken couscous salad 110
     chicken laksa 82
     chicken, leek and sweetcorn
          cobbler 28
     Chinese chicken 128
     garlic chicken casserole 154
     huntsman chicken 166
     lemongrass and lime herby chicken
          kebabs 42
     lemon thyme chicken with summer
          vegetables 99
     orange and basil chicken 121
     spring chicken bake 85
     warm chicken salad with lemon
          dressing 73

chick pea salad, warm spinach and 86
chilli, quick chorizo and bean 120
Chinese chicken 128
Chinese stir fried pork 140
Chinese vegetables, stir fried 155
Christmas cranberry muffins 18
chocolate:
     banana and chocolate muffins 60
     chocolate Hallowe'en cupcakes 158
     chocolate, rum and raisin pudding 75
chorizo and bean chilli, quick 120
cinnamon apple flan 157
citrus crusted salmon 72
clementine pavlova, jewelled 32
cookies, orange sweetheart 47
couscous salad, chicken 110
crab cakes with gingered cucumber,
     Thai style 111
cranberry muffins, Christmas 18
creamy celeriac soup 22
creamy gooseberry fool 103
creamy ham and mushroom pasta 163
creamy smoked mackerel pasta 150
creamy summery pasta 96
crisp coated fish with chips 52
cucumber, Thai style crab cakes with
     gingered 111
cupcakes, chocolate Hallowe'en 158
curried parsnip soup 36
curries:
     beef rogan josh 38
     cheat's chicken makhani 54
     chicken laksa 82
     kofta in red curry sauce 152
     potato and spinach curry (saag aloo) 66
custard pots, baked nutmeg 173

D
desserts:
     athol brose with nectarines 130
     Baileys mousse 17
     baked nutmeg custard pots 173
     baked pears with honey, nutmeg and
          lemon 145
     chocolate, rum and raisin pudding 75
     cinnamon apple flan 157
     creamy gooseberry fool 103
     fruity cinnamon rice pudding 172
     jewelled clementine pavlova 32
     lemon and ginger sponge puddings 89
     lemon meringue pie 61
     plum charlotte 144
     rum caramelised oranges 33

summer fruit frozen yogurt 131
dumplings, winter vegetable casserole with spicy 14

E
Easter Sunday roast lamb with thyme and mint gravy 64
easy apricot scones 117

F
fish:
    baked haddock with tomatoes 168
    Cajun fish cakes 68
    citrus crusted salmon 72
    creamy smoked mackerel pasta 150
    crisp coated fish with chips 52
    fish pie 26
    Italian fish stew 44
    Mediterranean baked fish 84
    smoked mackerel and potato salad 114
    smoked salmon pâté 9
    tuna salad filling 129
fool, creamy gooseberry 103
fruit:
    athol brose with nectarines 130
    baked pears with honey, nutmeg and lemon 145
    blueberry hotcakes 106
    cinnamon apple flan 157
    creamy gooseberry fool 103
    fruity cinnamon rice pudding 172
    jewelled clementine pavlova 32
    plum charlotte 144
    rum caramelised oranges 33
    summer fruit frozen yogurt 131

G
gammon in raisin sauce 29
garden herb soup 107
garlic chicken casserole 154
garlicky mushroom soup 134
gooseberry fool, creamy 103
gratins:
    autumn vegetable gratin 169
    baked marrow gratin 138
gremolata, summer stew with 108

H
haddock with tomatoes, baked 168
Hallowe'en hubble bubble casserole 156
ham:
    creamy ham and mushroom pasta 163
    warm broad bean and smoked ham pittas 92
harvest gold soup 148
herb soup, garden 107
honey and mustard pork 13

honey and sultana drop scones 74
hotcakes, blueberry 106
huntsman chicken 166

I
Italian fish stew 44

J
jewelled clementine pavlova 32

K
kebabs, lemongrass and lime herby chicken 42
kofta in red curry sauce 152

L
lamb:
    baked marrow gratin 138
    Easter Sunday roast lamb with thyme and mint gravy 64
    lamb koftas with mint dip 81
    minty lamb burgers 113
    navarin of lamb 88
    rosemary redcurrant lamb 125
leeks:
    asparagus and leek tart 78
    chicken, leek and sweetcorn cobbler 28
    St David's Day leek and mustard potato tart 57
    sweet potato, leek and tomato soup 162
lemongrass and lime herby chicken kebabs 42
lemon and ginger sponge puddings 89
lemon meringue pie 61
lemon thyme chicken with summer vegetables 99

M
mackerel:
    creamy smoked mackerel pasta 150
    smoked mackerel and potato salad 114
marrow gratin, baked 138
meatballs, spicy Swedish 80
Mediterranean baked fish 84
Mexican tortillas with spicy beef 126
minty lamb burgers 113
mousse, Baileys 17
muffins:
    banana and chocolate muffins 60
    Christmas cranberry muffins 18
mushrooms:
    chicken and mushroom pie 136
    creamy ham and mushroom pasta 163
    garlicky mushroom soup 134
mussels, Thai style 56

N
navarin of lamb 88
nectarines, athol brose with 130

O
one pot Italian beef stew 135
onions:
    bangers and mash with onion gravy 164
    peppered steak with balsamic onions 24
oranges:
    orange and basil chicken 121
    orange sweetheart cookies 47
    rum caramelised oranges 33
orecchiette with pork ragù 67
Oriental style turkey leftovers 12

P
pancakes with garlic prawns, shrimp 98
parsnip soup, curried 36
pasta:
    cannelloni 40
    creamy ham and mushroom pasta 163
    creamy smoked mackerel pasta 150
    creamy summery pasta 96
    one pot Italian beef stew 135
    orecchiette with pork ragù 67
    pastrami and ricotta pasta 116
    St Valentine's Day seafood and tomato pasta 46
    spiced cauliflower pasta 25
    sunshine spaghetti 124
pastrami and ricotta pasta 116
pâté, smoked salmon 9
pavlova, jewelled clementine 32
pears with honey, nutmeg and lemon, baked 145
peppered steak with balsamic onions 24
pies, savoury:
    chicken and mushroom pie 136
    fish pie 26
    vegetarian shepherd's pie 53
pies, sweet:
    lemon meringue pie 61
pineapple burgers, spicy pork and 70
plum charlotte 144
pork:
    bangers and mash with onion gravy 164
    braised pork casserole 15
    cannelloni 40
    Chinese stir fried pork 140
    Hallowe'en hubble bubble casserole 156

honey and mustard pork 13
orecchiette with pork ragù 67
pork tenderloin with rhubarb
    chutney 50
spare ribs 112
spicy pork and pineapple burgers 70
winter pork ragù 30
potato, leek and tomato soup
    sweet 162
potatoes:
    bangers and mash with onion
        gravy 164
    crisp coated fish with chips 52
    navarin of lamb 88
    potato and spinach curry (saag aloo) 66
    St David's Day leek and mustard potato
        tart 57
    smoked mackerel and potato salad 114
prune casserole, rich beef and 170

Q
quick chorizo and bean chilli 120

R
raisin sauce, gammon in 29
redcurrant lamb, rosemary 125
rice pudding, fruity cinnamon 172
rich beef and prune casserole 170
risotto:
    risotto of summer vegetables 95
    saffron seafood risotto 142
roast beef with Yorkshires 41
rosemary redcurrant lamb 125
rum and raisin pudding, chocolate 75
rum caramelised oranges 33

S
saag aloo (potato and spinach curry) 66
saffron seafood risotto 142
St David's Day leek and mustard potato
    tart 57
St Valentine's Day seafood and tomato
    pasta 46
salads:
    chicken couscous salad 110
    sesame beef salad 94
    smoked mackerel and potato salad 114
    tuna salad filling 129
    warm chicken salad with lemon
        dressing 73
    warm spinach and chick pea salad 86
salmon:
    citrus crusted salmon 72
    smoked salmon pâté 9

sausages:
    bangers and mash with onion
        gravy 164
    Hallowe'en hubble bubble
        casserole 156
scones:
    easy apricot scones 117
    honey and sultana drop scones 74
seafood:
    fish pie 26
    Italian fish stew 44
    saffron seafood risotto 142
    St Valentine's Day seafood and tomato
        pasta 46
    shrimp pancakes with garlic
        prawns 98
    Thai style crab cakes with gingered
        cucumber 111
    Thai style mussels 56
sesame beef salad 94
shepherd's pie, vegetarian 53
shrimp pancakes with garlic prawns 98
smoked mackerel and potato salad 114
smoked salmon pâté 9
soufflé, cheese and corn 141
soups:
    chestnut soup with sage and caraway
        croûtons 8
    creamy celeriac soup 22
    curried parsnip soup 36
    garden herb soup 107
    garlicky mushroom soup 134
    harvest gold soup 148
    sweet potato, leek and tomato
        soup 162
spare ribs 112
spiced cauliflower pasta 25
spicy pork and pineapple burgers 70
spicy Swedish meatballs 80
spinach:
    potato and spinach curry 66
    warm spinach and chick pea salad 86
spring chicken bake 85
squash and goat's cheese strudel,
    butternut 151
steak:
    peppered steak with balsamic
        onions 24
stews:
    Italian fish stew 44
    one pot Italian beef stew 135
    summer stew with gremolata 108
stir fried chinese vegetables 155
stir fried pork, chinese 140
strudel, butternut squash and goat's
    cheese 151

summer fruit frozen yogurt 131
summer stew with gremolata 108
sunshine spaghetti 124
sweetcorn:
    cheese and corn soufflé 141
    chicken, leek and sweetcorn
        cobbler 28
sweet potato, leek and tomato soup 162

T
tandoori chicken, butterflied 100
tarts:
    asparagus and leek tart 78
    cinnamon apple flan 157
    St David's Day leek and mustard potato
        tart 57
Thai style crab cakes with gingered
    cucumber 111
Thai style mussels 56
tomatoes:
    baked haddock with tomatoes 168
    sweet potato, leek and tomato
        soup 162
tortillas with spicy beef, Mexican 126
tuna salad filling 129
turkey leftovers, Oriental style 12

V
vegetables:
    aubergine parmigiana 122
    autumn vegetable gratin 169
    chicken and spring vegetable
        fricassee 71
    creamy summery pasta 96
    lemon thyme chicken with summer
        vegetables 99
    risotto of summer vegetables 95
    stir fried Chinese vegetables 155
    summer stew with gremolata 108
    winter vegetable casserole with spicy
        dumplings 14
vegetarian shepherd's pie 53

W
warm broad bean and smoked ham
    pittas 92
warm chicken salad with lemon
    dressing 73
warm spinach and chick pea salad 86
winter pork ragù 30
winter vegetable casserole with spicy
    dumplings 14

Y
yogurt, summer fruit frozen 131
Yorkshires, roast beef with 41